B53 025 669 5

D0533498

ROTHERHAM LIBRARY & INFORM

SWI

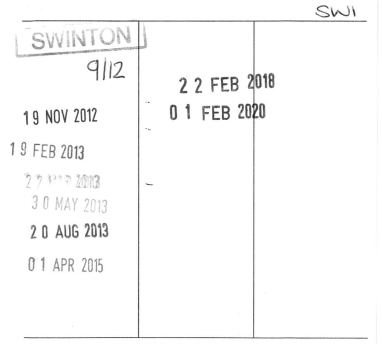

SWINTON

9/12

19 NOV 2012

1 9 FEB 2013

2 2 MAR 2013

3 0 MAY 2013

2 0 AUG 2013

0 1 APR 2015

2 2 FEB 2018

0 1 FEB 2020

This book must be returned by the date specified at the time of issue as the DATE DUE FOR RETURN.

The loan may be extended (personally, by post, telephone or online) for a further period if the book is not required by another reader, by quoting the above number / author / title.

Enquiries: 01709 336774

www.rotherham.gov.uk/libraries

Other books by Sarah Flower:

THE EVERYDAY HALOGEN OVEN COOKBOOK
Quick, easy and nutritious recipes for all the family

SLOW COOK, FAST FOOD
Over 250 healthy, wholesome slow cooker and one pot meals for all the family

PERFECT BAKING WITH YOUR HALOGEN OVEN
How to create tasty bread, cupcakes, bakes, biscuits and savouries

THE EVERYDAY HALOGEN FAMILY COOKBOOK
Another 200 delicious meals and treats from the author of The Everyday Halogen Oven Cookbook

EAT WELL, SPEND LESS
The complete guide to everyday family cooking

HALOGEN COOKING FOR TWO

THE HEALTHY LIVING DIET COOKBOOK

For advice about everyday cooking visit www.everydaycookery.com and for more tips and advice on using your halogen oven visit www.everydayhalogen.com

Write or phone for a catalogue to:

How To Books
Spring Hill House
Spring Hill Road
Begbroke
Oxford
OX5 1RX
Tel. 01865 375794

Or email: info@howtobooks.co.uk

Visit our website www.howtobooks.co.uk to find out more about us and our books.

Like our Facebook page **How To Books & Spring Hill**

Follow us on **Twitter@Howtobooksltd**

Read our books online www.howto.co.uk

HALOGEN
One Pot Cooking

SARAH FLOWER

SPRING HILL

Published by Spring Hill, an imprint of How To Books Ltd.
Spring Hill House, Spring Hill Road
Begbroke, Oxford OX5 1RX
United Kingdom
Tel: (01865) 375794
Fax: (01865) 379162
info@howtobooks.co.uk
www.howtobooks.co.uk

First published 2012

How To Books greatly reduce the carbon footprint of their books
by sourcing their typesetting and printing in the UK.

All rights reserved. No part of this work may be reproduced or stored in an
information retrieval system (other than for purposes of review) without the
express permission of the publisher in writing.

The right of Sarah Flower to be identified as author of this work has
been asserted by her in accordance with the Copyright, Designs and Patents
Act 1988.

Text © 2012 Sarah Flower

British Library Cataloguing in Publication Data
A catalogue record of this book is available from the British Library.

ISBN: 978 1 905862 64 1

Illustrations by Firecatcher Creative
Produced for How To Books by Deer Park Productions, Tavistock, Devon
Typeset by TW Typesetting, Plymouth, Devon
Printed and bound by in Great Britain by Bell & Bain Ltd, Glasgow

NOTE: The material contained in this book is set out in good faith for general
guidance and no liability can be accepted for loss or expense incurred as a
result of relying in particular circumstances on statements made in the book.
Laws and regulations are complex and liable to change, and readers should
check the current position with relevant authorities before making personal
arrangements.

Contents

Introduction

It was suggested by my publishers that there would be a market for one-pot halogen recipes – so here is the book! One pot describes how you serve the meal, such as a lasagne dish or shepherd's pie. It does not mean you can cook the whole meal only using only one pot. Sometimes for a casserole or stew it is possible, but I prefer to brown the meat in a sauté pan first.

This book has some old favourites as well as new recipes I hope you will enjoy. As with all my halogen books, I have included a chapter on how to use your halogen – feel free to ignore this if you already know the basics, though sometimes it is good to have a bit of a revise.

I hope you enjoy the recipes. Remember you can contact me via the website www.sarahflower.co.uk or visit my halogen website www.everydayhalogen.com where you will find new recipes, tips, reviews, advice and can even join in the forums.

Enjoy!

Sarah x

Using Your Halogen Oven

As in my other halogen cookbooks, this first chapter shows newbie halogen oven users how to get the most from their machine. If you have bought another one of my books, you may want to skip this chapter as it contains duplicate information.

Choosing the right machine for you

There are many different halogen ovens on the market, but they are basically all the same machine. The two main variations are the bowl size and whether your lid is on a hinge. My first machine was from JML when they first started to become popular. I was not really sure what to expect and, over time, it has gained more and more use in our home. Personally I would opt for the largest bowl as this increases the oven's usability. You can also purchase extenders, which can help maximise use. Extenders are metal rings that fit over the top of the halogen bowl, literally extending the height of the bowl and enabling you to fit more into your oven. The lid then fits on top of the extender. They are also useful if you want to keep the food away from the heating elements to prevent burning.

After using the JML, I progressed to the Flavorwave Turbo Platinum Oven. Some of the advantages of this particular oven are that it has a hinged lid, digital settings, three-speed fan and a pre-heat setting. At the time of writing I reviewed Lakeland's Visicook Crisp and Bake Halogen Oven. It is pricier than other halogens, but I like the sleek black finish, the food tumbler system (which I have never seen on any other halogen) and the fact that it comes with the extender ring as standard. Just like the Flavorwave, the Visicook comes with a hinged lid which is much better than the cheaper halogens that don't have this feature. It does not have a digital clock which is a bit of a shame, but nonetheless, it is a good machine. The food tumbler system works in the same way as the ActiFry fryer so it is a great tool if you like cooking food such as potato wedges or chips.

Looking at online forums I have noticed that the lids are a bit of a bugbear. I used a lid stand positioned beside my JML machine, though annoyingly these are optional extras that you have to purchase and are quite flimsy to look at. Personally, I think it is better to buy the halogen cooker with the hinged lid if you can afford it – this is definitely a safer and easier option.

How do they work?

The halogen oven is basically a large glass bowl with an electric halogen lid. The lid is heavy as it contains the halogen element, timer and temperature settings. It can be fiddly to clean but I will come to that later. The halogen bulbs heat up the bowl and the fan moves the air around the bowl to create an even temperature. As it is smaller than a conventional oven, it heats up faster, reducing the need for long preheating and in some cases reducing the overall cooking time.

This makes it a very popular choice for those watching their pennies, living on their own or, like me, cooking for a busy family. It has even become a popular choice for students and caravanners. I read on a forum that some caravanners use the self-clean facility just like a mini dishwasher – ingenious! It is also popular as a second oven and really becomes invaluable at busy times like Christmas.

For safety, the lid's handle has to be in place (placed securely down) for the machine to turn on. This means that when you lift the lid, the oven is automatically turned off. If you are using the Flavorwave machine with the hinged lid, you have to press the start button and remember to turn the machine off when you lift the lid.

The halogen does cook slightly differently to a conventional oven, so first beginning to use it often involves a process of trial and error, but it is not vastly different. If you have favourite recipes that you cook in the conventional oven, try them in the halogen. I find cooking at a slightly lower temperature or cooking for less time normally gives the same results, but hopefully this book will help give you more confidence.

The halogen oven is not a microwave and does not work in the same way as a microwave, so if you are thinking you can cook food in minutes you are wrong. It does, however, have a multitude of functions – defrosting, baking, grilling, roasting and steaming are all perfect for the halogen. Remember that to get the optimum benefit, air needs to circulate around the bowl, so ideally place dishes and trays on racks and avoid the temptation to over fill.

Getting the right equipment

This sounds obvious but . . . make sure you have oven trays, baking sheets and casserole dishes that will fit inside your halogen oven. There is nothing more frustrating than planning a meal and just at the last minute realising that your dish does not fit in the machine! You can use any ovenproof dish or tray – metal, silicon and Pyrex are all fine. The halogen oven is round so it makes sense to look at trays and stands of the same shape, just smaller so you can remove them without burning yourself!

Out of everything, I think this is the halogen's biggest downfall. When I first started using one, it was frustrating to find that 80% of my bakeware did not fit in the machine but a quick revamp and purchase of the accessories have proved invaluable. If money is tight, you will often find great casserole dishes at boot sales or charity shops – you don't have to spend a fortune on new cookware.

You can also buy an accessories pack, which contains steamer pans, grilling pans, toasting racks and even an extension ring. These are highly recommended if you use your oven regularly and certainly enhance what you can do with the machine. There are many websites selling or advertising these accessories, so a general internet search will point you in the right direction. Amazon is also a great place to look.

Let there be light

As experienced halogen users will know, the halogen light turns on and off during cooking. This is not a fault of the thermostat as some people have mentioned on forums. It literally turns off when the programmed temperature is reached, then on again when it drops. Set the temperature and marvel at how quickly the oven reaches the required temperature – literally in minutes. I love the light – along with being able to watch your food cook, there is something quite cosy about walking into your kitchen on a winter or autumn evening and seeing the glow of the halogen cooker.

Timings

The halogen oven comes with a 60-minute timer and temperature-setting dials. The Flavorwave Turbo also comes with three fan settings and a digital timer. All halogens turn off when the timer settings have been reached. This means that you can be reassured that if the phone rings or you are called away from the kitchen, your food won't spoil.

Size

The oven is small enough to sit on a worktop, but do allow space for removal of the lid if it is not hinged. The lid can get very hot and is quite large and heavy, being the brains of the machine, so it can be a good idea to buy the lid stand. However, be careful when using this stand as it can seem quite flimsy until you get used to it. You could opt to place the lid on a heatproof surface but, again, be careful not to burn yourself or your worktop!

Careful does it

Your oven should come with a tong type of gadget to help you lift out the racks. They are quite useful, but I also use a more substantial set of tongs. As with any oven or cooker, do be careful as the bowl and contents get very hot. I find using proper oven gloves a necessity as they cover your whole hand and wrist and can prevent accidents.

As with all electrical and hot appliances, do not let your children near the halogen – the glass bowl gets very hot.

Foil and coverings

Some people like to use foil when cooking. This can be a good idea as it prevents food from browning too quickly or it can be used to parcel foods, but make sure the foil is secure. The fan is very strong and if the foil is not secure it could float around the oven and might damage the element. Another option for preventing burning is obviously to turn the temperature down or place the food further away from the element (use the low rack or add an extension ring).

Cleaning your oven

Your oven is promoted as being self-cleaning. This basically means that you fill it with a little water and a squirt of washing-up liquid and then turn it on to the wash setting. The combination of the fan and the heat allows the water to swish around the bowl giving it a quick clean. This normally takes about 10 minutes. Personally I find it just as simple to remove the bowl and place it in the dishwasher – it always comes out gleaming.

The lid is a little more difficult to clean and I would refer to the manufacturer's guidelines as each product differs a little. Do not get the element or electrical parts wet!

High and low racks

There are two standard racks which come with every halogen oven – a high and a low rack (not to be confused with the rack I use for grilling!). The high rack is nearer the element so use this more if you want to brown something. The low rack is used more for longer cooking times.

You can cook directly on the bottom of the bowl. It does cook well but takes a little longer compared with using the racks, as air is not able to circulate all around the food.

Grilling

If you want to grill something you really need to place the rack as high as possible. The two racks (low and high) that come with the halogen oven may not be suitable for quick grilling – though if this is all you have it will work, but just take longer. I purchased an accessory pack and in this you get a toasting rack (with egg holes), which can be used as a grilling rack, either on its own or with a baking tray on top.

As you are cooking close to the element, grilling times are much quicker, for example you can grill cheese on toast in approximately 3–4 minutes.

Baking

Some people worry about using the halogen to bake cakes but I think this is because they are setting the oven temperature too high, resulting in a crusty brown cake top with a soggy middle. Setting the oven to a lower temperature can solve this problem. Muffins and cupcakes take between 12 and 18 minutes. You only really encounter problems with cakes if you are cooking for too long at too high a temperature. Try some of my cake recipes and you will see how simple it can be.

Preheat or not to preheat

Most recipes I have found on forums don't mention preheating the oven. This is probably due to how quickly the oven reaches its temperature setting. However, I think it is worth turning the oven on a few minutes before use just to bring it up to the right temperature if you are baking cakes.

I found this to be the case when attempting to cook soft-boiled eggs. According to the Flavorwave recipe book, I should be able to cook a soft egg in 6 minutes just by placing it on the high rack. It didn't work, but when I tried again in a heated oven it was much more successful.

Some machines (such as the Flavorwave) have a preheat button which preheats at 260°C for 6 minutes, but others, such as the JML, require you to set the oven to the required temperature and then turn it on.

I hope this chapter has not confused you. Move on to try some recipes and then come back to this chapter at a later date – it will probably make more sense then!

Enjoy!

Conversion charts
This book provides metric measurements, but those who still prefer Imperial, or who want to use US measures, can use these conversions.

WEIGHT	
Metric	**Imperial**
25g	1oz
50g	2oz
75g	3oz
100g	4oz
150g	5oz
175g	6oz
200g	7oz
225g	8oz
250g	9oz
300g	10oz
350g	12oz
400g	14oz
450g	1lb

OVEN TEMPERATURES	
Celsius	**Fahrenheit**
110°C	225°F
120°C	250°F
140°C	275°F
150°C	300°F
160°C	325°F
180°C	350°F
190°C	375°F
200°C	400°F
220°C	425°F
230°C	450°F
240°C	475°F

LIQUIDS		
Metric	**Imperial**	**US cup**
5ml	1 tsp	1 tsp
15ml	1 tbsp	1 tbsp
50ml	2fl oz	3 tbsp
60ml	$2\frac{1}{2}$fl oz	$\frac{1}{4}$ cup
75ml	3fl oz	$\frac{1}{3}$ cup
100ml	4fl oz	scant $\frac{1}{2}$ cup
125ml	$4\frac{1}{2}$fl oz	$\frac{1}{2}$ cup
150ml	5fl oz	$\frac{2}{3}$ cup
200ml	7fl oz	scant 1 cup
250ml	10fl oz	1 cup
300ml	$\frac{1}{2}$pt	$1\frac{1}{4}$ cups
350ml	12fl oz	$1\frac{1}{3}$ cups
400ml	$\frac{3}{4}$pt	$1\frac{3}{4}$ cups
500ml		2 cups
600ml	1pt	$2\frac{1}{2}$ cups

MEASUREMENTS	
Metric	**Imperial**
5cm	2in
10cm	4in
13cm	5in
15cm	6in
18cm	7in
20cm	8in
25cm	10in
30cm	12in

Poultry

This chapter includes mainly chicken recipes but does include some recipes for turkey and even pheasant if you are feeling adventurous. Chicken seems to be the favourite of most families, and kids love it. Chicken thighs give more flavour and you can buy boneless fillets. If you are watching your weight, remember to remove any visible fat or skin before cooking. Quorn is a great substitute for chicken, it is low fat and also suitable for vegetarians – most of the chicken recipes in this chapter will work well with Quorn.

Serves 4

Simple Coq Au Vin

Preparation time:
10 minutes
Cooking time:
50 minutes

A quick and easy variation on the traditional French favourite.

- Score the chicken breasts or thighs before rubbing with olive oil and sprinkling with paprika and seasoning. Place in a deep ovenproof dish that has been drizzled with olive oil. Add the shallots, garlic and lardons and place in the halogen on the high rack. Cook at 200°C for 15 minutes.

- Add the butter and cook for another 5–8 minutes, ensuring everything is combined.

- Remove from the oven. Remove the chicken and place to one side.

- Sprinkle the flour into the dish to soak up any juices before adding a little of the wine, stirring to ensure it is combined. Then add the remaining wine, port, chicken stock and tomatoes.

- Add the bay leaves and thyme, season well and then add the chicken and mushrooms, making sure they are submerged in the stock.

- Return to the halogen oven and cook for another 30 minutes.

- Serve with sauté or mashed potatoes and green vegetables.

Ingredients:
4–6 chicken pieces (breast or
    thigh, whatever you prefer)
Olive oil
Paprika
Seasoning
12 shallots, left whole
3–4 cloves garlic, thickly
    sliced
200g smoked lardons
25g butter
1 tablespoon flour
200ml red wine
200ml port
300ml chicken stock
3 tomatoes, finely chopped
2 bay leaves
2–3 sprigs thyme
200g button mushrooms

Serves 4

Italian Chicken Pot Roast

Ingredients:

2 red onions, cut into thick wedges/slices

2 red peppers, cut into thick wedges/slices

2 courgettes, cut into thick slices

½ aubergine, cut into thick slices

2 sweet potatoes, not peeled but cut into thick slices

12–16 cherry tomatoes, left whole

8–10 olives (optional)

Olive oil

1 tablespoon balsamic vinegar

Sea salt

Black pepper

Approx. ¼ teaspoon sugar

4 chicken breasts

Paprika

3–4 sprigs rosemary or thyme

A really simple yet delicious pot roast, perfect for when you want a great meal with little effort.

- Place the vegetables in a bowl. Drizzle over some olive oil (about 2 tablespoons) and the balsamic vinegar. Mix well with your hands, ensuring everything is evenly coated.

- Pour the vegetables into your roasting tin (first making sure it fits in your halogen!). Sprinkle with sea salt, black pepper and sugar.

- Rub your chicken breasts with olive oil. Place them in the roasting tin with the vegetables, either on top or in amongst the vegetables if you have room.

- Sprinkle the chicken breasts with paprika – this adds flavour but also helps give a nice golden colour. Place the herbs in amongst the chicken and vegetables.

- Place in the halogen on the low rack and roast at 200°C for 15 minutes. Remove and turn the chicken, adding more oil or paprika if needed.

- Place back in the oven and cook for another 15–20 minutes or until the chicken is cooked.

- Poultry

Italian Chicken Casserole

Preparation time:
10 minutes
Cooking time:
45-50 minutes

You can also make a veggie version of this by substituting Quorn fillets for the chicken.

- In a large sauté pan, fry the onion and garlic in a dash of olive oil for 2 minutes. Add the red pepper and cook for another 2 minutes.

- Add the chicken, pancetta or bacon and paprika. Stir, cooking gently for 5 minutes.

- Add all the remaining ingredients. Cook for another couple of minutes.

- Pour this into a casserole dish that fits in the halogen oven. Cover the dish with a lid and cook at 180°C for 35–40 minutes.

- Serve with small roast or sauté potatoes and vegetables.

Ingredients:
Olive oil
1 onion
2-3 cloves garlic, crushed
1 red pepper, diced
4 chicken breasts, fillets or pieces
3-4 rashers pancetta or bacon, diced
2 teaspoons paprika
1 tin chopped tomatoes
2 teaspoons sundried tomato paste
200ml red wine
200ml stock or water
80g button mushrooms, halved
Small handful of fresh basil, chopped
Seasoning to taste

Preparation time:
10 minutes

Cooking time:
45–50 minutes

Serves 4

Chicken and Mushroom Casserole

Ingredients:
A drizzle or spray of olive oil
1–2 cloves garlic
2 leeks, finely chopped
6 spring onions, finely
    chopped
300g chicken pieces (you can
    use cooked chicken)
125g mushrooms
200ml white wine
300ml chicken stock
1 teaspoon cornflour
1 teaspoon paprika
100g French beans
1 teaspoon dried tarragon (or
    a handful of fresh tarragon)

Perfect for a warming supper – I love the flavours in this casserole.
I normally serve with minted new potatoes or roasted new potatoes.

- Heat a little olive oil in a sauté pan and cook the garlic, leeks and spring onions for 2–3 minutes. Add the chicken and mushrooms and cook for a further 5 minutes.

- Place the chicken mixture in your casserole dish (first making sure it fits in the halogen). Add the wine and stock to the dish.

- Mix the cornflour with 10ml water in a cup to form a smooth paste and add to the chicken pot.

- Add all the remaining ingredients. If you are using fresh tarragon, add half now and retain half to add in the last 10 minutes of cooking.

- Place in the halogen and cook at 180°C for 35–40 minutes. If the casserole starts to form a skin on the top you can pop on the casserole lid, or securely wrap a piece of tin foil over the top of the dish.

> **Top Tip**: If you prefer a creamier sauce, add some low-fat Greek yoghurt or low-fat crème fraîche 5 minutes before serving.

● **Poultry**

Serves 4

Preparation time:
10–15 minutes
Cooking time:
30–35 minutes

Cashew, Walnut and Mushroom Stuffed Chicken

Cashews work so well with mushrooms. This recipe happened by chance when I was looking for something to do with chicken and had some leftover nut roast – it tasted amazing so I worked on the recipe. Hope you enjoy it.

Ingredients:
30g cashew nuts
30g walnuts
80g chestnut mushrooms
1 onion
2–3 cloves garlic, finely
   chopped
½–1 teaspoon Marmite
4 chicken breasts
8 rashers pancetta
Olive oil
Seasoning

- If you have a food processor, this is the best and quickest way to make the dish. Use it to finely chop the cashew nuts, walnuts, mushrooms and onion. Place in a bowl and mix in the garlic.

- Combine well and add the Marmite, mixing to ensure it is evenly distributed.

- With a sharp knife, cut a slit in the side of each chicken breast to form a pocket. Stuff the mixture into these pockets. Wrap around the pancetta to secure.

- Place the chicken breasts on a greased ovenproof dish. Drizzle with a little olive oil and season.

- Place in the halogen on the low rack and cook at 200°C for 25–30 minutes until the chicken is cooked.

Serves 4

Crusty Red Pesto Chicken

Ingredients:
4 chicken breasts
4–6 tablespoons low-fat
  cream cheese or quark
2–4 tablespoons red pesto
50g wholemeal breadcrumbs
25g oats
25g mixed nuts, finely
  chopped
25g Parmesan cheese
Black pepper
Olive oil

You can prepare the chicken in advance and bake when needed. Remember to bring the chicken back to room temperature before baking.

- Cut each chicken breast with a sharp knife to form a pocket.

- Mix the cream cheese or quark with the pesto.

- Place a little in each chicken breast – don't overstuff as it will come out when cooking. Place on an oiled baking tray or tin.

- In a bowl, mix the breadcrumbs, oats, nuts and Parmesan together. Season to taste.

- Rub the chicken breasts with olive oil and then press down a handful of the breadcrumb mixture over each breast.

- Drizzle with a little more olive oil before placing in the halogen on the low rack. Set to 190°C and cook for 20–30 minutes until the chicken is cooked through perfectly.

- Serve with salad.

Serves 4

Cajun Chicken with Roasted Sweet Potatoes

Preparation time:
10 minutes
Cooking time:
30 minutes

I love the Cajun flavour – you can buy Cajun flavouring from the spice section in your supermarket which is far easier than mixing together your own spices. Sweet potatoes work so well with a spiced dish, and you get loads of antioxidants too.

Ingredients:
6 sweet potatoes, cut into
   thick wedges (skins left on)
2 red onions, cut into wedges
Olive oil
Paprika
Sea salt
Black pepper
4-6 chicken breasts
2-3 tablespoons Cajun spice
1 tablespoon runny honey
Juice and zest of 1 lime

- Place the sweet potato and onion in an ovenproof dish and sprinkle with olive oil. Toss to ensure they are evenly coated. Sprinkle with paprika, sea salt and black pepper.

- Place in the halogen on the high rack and cook at 200°C for 10 minutes.

- Meanwhile, score the chicken breasts with a sharp knife. Combine the Cajun spice with the honey and lime juice and zest and, using a pastry brush, coat the chicken breasts thoroughly.

- Remove the tray from the halogen and add the chicken breasts to the potato and onion wedges. If you have Cajun mixture leftover, you can also coat the potatoes.

- Return to the high rack and cook for another 20–25 minutes, or until the chicken is cooked thoroughly.

- Serve with green salad.

Serves 4–6

Whole Chicken Casserole

Ingredients:
1 whole chicken, prepared and
    ready to cook
1 lemon, halved
Olive oil
250g shallots
3–4 cloves garlic, roughly
    chopped
4 carrots, thickly diced
4 sticks celery, thickly sliced
2 sweet potatoes, thickly
    diced
3 large potatoes, thickly diced
2 leeks, thickly sliced
4 tomatoes, diced
2–3 sprigs thyme
1–2 teaspoons paprika
Seasoning to taste
500ml chicken stock (extra
    stock may be needed)
500ml white wine or
    vermouth

This is a very simple dish and perfect for that satisfying dinner. If you have a digital halogen, you can preset the timer to suit. However, if you have a halogen with a manual timer, such as the JML oven, you will be able to cook for only 1 hour at a time and then you will need to adjust the timer when required.

- Prepare the chicken for cooking (make sure it fits easily in your halogen!). Place the two lemon halves into the cavity of the chicken and rub the skin with olive oil.

- Place the chicken, breast down, into the halogen, directly onto the base of the bowl.

- Place the vegetables around the chicken, ensuring they are evenly distributed. Finish with the thyme and sprinkle with the paprika. Season to taste.

- Heat the stock gently on your hob, add the wine or vermouth and pour this around the chicken.

- Cook for 30 minutes at 180°C.

- Remove the chicken gently. Stir around the vegetables, adding more chicken stock if necessary.

- Place the chicken back in the oven breast-side up. You may need to wiggle the chicken around to make sure the vegetables don't get trapped beneath it. Sprinkle the breast with a little more paprika and thyme and season and cook at the same temperature for

- **Poultry**

another 45–60 minutes until the chicken is cooked to taste. The cooking time depends on the size of the chicken and personal taste.

- To serve, carve the chicken and spoon over the vegetable and stock mixture. Enjoy!

Top Tip: To make very crispy, tasty roast potatoes, the key is to use very hot oil – goose-fat is one of the best fats to use. I cut my potatoes at angles – one large potato can normally cut into three roast potatoes. Don't cut them too small as you want crispy potatoes with a nice fluffy middle. Try to make sure the potatoes are all roughly the same size so they cook evenly. Place the fat in the oven so it starts to get hot. Parboil your potatoes for approximately 10 minutes. The outer edge of the potato should start to soften. Drain and place the potatoes back into the empty saucepan. Add a generous sprinkle of paprika and semolina. Pop on the saucepan lid, holding it down firmly, shake the saucepan to bash the potatoes. Remove the roasting tin from the oven and carefully, using tongs, add the potatoes to the hot fat. It will spit and bubble so be careful not to splash. Once the potatoes are in the fat, you can turn them gently as this ensures the fat is adhered to all sides of the potato before cooking. Sprinkle with a little more paprika and semolina if needed. Place back in the oven and cook at 200°C until they are golden. Halfway through cooking I turn them and drain off any excess oil.

Ingredients:
15–20 small shallots, peeled
  (or 2 onions, diced)
2–3 cloves garlic, roughly
  chopped
500g chicken thigh fillets
150g cubed thick pancetta
  (cubetti di pancetta)
Olive oil
1 tablespoon butter
100g button mushrooms
400ml white wine
300ml chicken stock
1 small handful of parsley,
  freshly chopped
1 bay leaf
Black pepper
2 teaspoons cornflour

Serves 4

Chicken in White Wine Sauce

Wine and chicken go so well together – this recipe is no exception. You could add a small handful of freshly chopped tarragon if you like the flavour.

- Place the shallots, garlic, chicken and pancetta in an ovenproof dish. Drizzle with olive oil and dot with the butter.

- Place in the halogen on the low rack and cook at 210°C for 15 minutes, turning the chicken occasionally.

- Remove from the oven and add all the remaining ingredients apart from the cornflour. Push the mushrooms down into the mixture as they have a tendency to bob around on the top and could become dry.

- Cover with a lid or double layer of foil, held securely. Place on the low rack and reduce the temperature to 190°C for 20 minutes.

- Mix the cornflour with a little water. Carefully pour this onto the liquid of the chicken dish, stirring to ensure it is evenly distributed. Cook for another 5–10 minutes as this helps thicken the sauce.

- Serve with sauté or mashed potatoes and green vegetables.

Serves 4

Creamy Chicken and Bacon Pasta Bake

Preparation time:
5–10 minutes
Cooking time:
25–30 minutes

This is a great supper, especially when you're in a hurry and have a big gap to fill. Teenagers love this dish. The health conscious can opt for wholewheat, spelt or rice/vegetable pasta.

- Cook the pasta as per the packet's instructions.

- Meanwhile, place the chicken, bacon and onion in an ovenproof dish. Drizzle with olive oil.

- Place in the halogen on the high rack and set the temperature to 200°C . Cook for 10 minutes before stirring and cooking for another 5–8 minutes until the chicken is cooked (the cooking time depends on the size of the chicken pieces).

- Add the remaining ingredients and stir well. Drain the pasta and add to the mixture. Add more milk and crème fraîche if you want a creamier or more liquid sauce. Combine well and season to taste.

- If you are a cheese addict, you could sprinkle some Cheddar over the top of the dish before baking.

- Place back in the halogen and cook for 10 more minutes before serving.

Ingredients:
200g pasta (e.g. penne)
3–4 chicken fillets, thickly diced
200g thick bacon or lardons, diced, or pancetta, cubed
1 large onion, diced
Olive oil
2 cloves garlic, crushed
150ml milk
350g low-fat crème fraîche
Small handful of fresh tarragon, finely chopped
Black pepper
Cheddar, grated (optional)

Serves 4

Chicken and Pepper One Pot

Ingredients:
4 chicken breasts, cut into
    large chunks
1 red onion, finely diced
2 cloves garlic, finely crushed
2–3 red peppers, thickly sliced
1 tin chopped tomatoes
2 tablespoons sundried
    tomato paste
Small handful of basil leaves,
    chopped
250ml vegetable or chicken
    stock, or red wine
½ teaspoon dried oregano
2 teaspoons paprika

A really simple dish that can be prepared in advance. Marinating improves the flavour of the chicken and produces a succulent, tasty dish.

- Place all the ingredients in an ovenproof dish and leave to marinate for 2–3 hours, covered, in the fridge.

- Remove the chicken from the fridge 1 hour before you want to cook to bring it back to room temperature.

- Place in the halogen on the low rack and set the temperature to 170°C. Cook for 30–35 minutes until the chicken is cooked.

- Serve with mini roast potatoes and green beans.

● **Poultry**

Serves 4

Preparation time:
15 minutes
Cooking time:
40–45 minutes

Golden Pheasant and Mushroom Bake

A lovely creamy, pheasant and mushroom base topped with a golden mash.

Ingredients:
4 potatoes
2 sweet potatoes
1 carrot
Seasoning
2 tablespoons butter
2 tablespoons plain flour
300ml chicken stock
100ml white wine
3–4 tablespoons single cream
½ teaspoon dried tarragon (or
   few sprigs of fresh, finely
   chopped)
Black pepper
Olive oil
1 onion, finely chopped
400g cooked pheasant,
   chopped
125g chestnut mushrooms,
   quartered

- Chop the potato, sweet potato and carrot into chunks. Boil or steam until soft. Drain and mash with a little butter and season to taste.

- While the potatoes are cooking you can prepare the rest of the dish. Melt the butter in a saucepan over a medium heat. Add the flour and stir for a few seconds to form a paste.

- Gradually add the chicken stock and white wine and keep stirring to form a sauce. Add the cream. If the sauce starts to go lumpy, use a balloon whisk and beat well. Cook until it thickens.

- Add the tarragon and black pepper. Leave to one side.

- Heat some olive oil in a sauté pan over a medium heat. Add the onion, cooked pheasant and the chestnut mushrooms. Cook until the mushrooms start to soften, then add the sauce. Heat through and pour into a deep ovenproof dish.

- Place the mashed mixture onto the pheasant base. You can pipe this on if you are feeling artistic. Use a fork and level out the top.

- When you are ready to cook, place on the low rack and set the temperature to 200°C. Cook for 20–25 minutes until the potato is golden.

- Serve with green vegetables.

Serves 4

Chicken, Bean and Tomato One Pot

Ingredients:
Olive oil
2 red onions, cut into small wedges
1 red pepper, sliced
3-4 cloves garlic, finely chopped
4 chicken breasts, halved
1 small punnet cherry tomatoes, left whole
Handful of fresh thyme (or 1-2 teaspoons of dried)
2 teaspoons paprika
450ml chicken stock
2-3 teaspoons sundried tomato purée
1 tin cannellini beans, drained
Seasoning to taste
Small handful of fresh parsley, finely chopped

Adding beans not only fills out this dish but can provide you with extra nutrients and energy, giving you the feeling of being fuller for longer.

- In a roasting tin or casserole dish that fits in your halogen, drizzle a little oil and add the onion, pepper, garlic, chicken and tomatoes. Drizzle with a little more oil ensuring everything is coated. Add the thyme and sprinkle with paprika.

- Place in the halogen on the low rack and cook at 200°C for 15 minutes.

- Remove from the halogen and add all the remaining ingredients. Combine well.

- Place back in the halogen and cook for another 20 minutes until the chicken is cooked to perfection.

- Poultry

Serves 4

Preparation time:
10 minutes

Cooking time:
35–40 minutes

Moroccan-style Chicken and Vegetable Casserole

I love using spices to create new dishes. This recipe uses a lot of spices, but allow them to infuse and the taste is amazing. If you don't like things too hot you can omit the chilli.

- Chop the chicken into chunks and place in a bowl.

- In a food processor, add 2 tablespoons olive oil, the spices, chilli, half the chopped herbs and the tomatoes. Whizz to form a marinade.

- Pour this onto the chicken and cover with clingfilm. Leave in the fridge to marinate overnight or for at least 2 hours. When you are ready to cook, bring it back up to room temperature for at least 1 hour.

- Place a little olive oil in your sauté pan over a medium heat. Add the onion, garlic and pepper and cook for 3–5 minutes before adding the chicken, holding back most of the marinade.

- Cook for 5 minutes before adding all the other ingredients, including the marinade.

- Simmer gently for 10 minutes before adding the remaining herbs. Then transfer to an ovenproof stock pot.

- Pop on a lid or double layer of foil. Place in the halogen on the low rack and cook at 180°C for 20–25 minutes.

- Serve with couscous.

Ingredients:
3–4 chicken fillets
Olive oil
2½cm knuckle of ginger, finely chopped
1 teaspoon paprika
1 teaspoon cumin
1 teaspoon turmeric
1 teaspoon cinnamon
1 small chilli
Small handful of mint leaves
Small handful of coriander leaves
3 tomatoes
1 red onion, finely chopped
2 cloves garlic, roughly chopped
1 red pepper, thickly diced
2 sweet potatoes, peeled and cut into chunks
1 carrot, diced
2 courgettes, thickly sliced
1 tin chickpeas, drained
1 tin chopped tomatoes
300ml chicken stock

Ingredients:
1 onion, finely chopped
2–3 cloves garlic, finely
    chopped
A spray of olive oil
1 pepper, finely chopped
    (optional)
400g turkey mince
150ml red wine
75g mushrooms, finely
    chopped (optional)
3–4 fresh tomatoes, chopped,
    or 1 tin chopped tomatoes
Mixed herbs to taste
Seasoning to taste

For the white sauce
25g butter
1 tablespoon plain flour or
    cornflour
500–750ml milk
¼ teaspoon mustard
    (optional)
Black pepper to taste
Sheets of lasagne (ensure the
    pack says 'no precooking
    required')
Grated cheese to garnish

Serves 4

Turkey Lasagne

This is a lighter version of the traditional beef lasagne – perfect if you are watching your weight (though opt for low-fat cheese and skimmed milk) but also if you are not a fan of red meats.

- Fry the onion and garlic in a little olive oil until soft and translucent. Add the pepper if you are including one.

- Add the mince and cook until brown, followed by the wine and mushrooms if using, and cook for 2 more minutes.

- Add the tinned or fresh tomatoes (or 'cheat' pasta sauce), stirring well. Finally, add the herbs and season to taste. Leave to simmer for 5 minutes.

- While the bolognese mix is simmering, make the white sauce. Melt the butter gently in a saucepan on a medium heat (not high!). Add the flour or cornflour and stir well with a wooden spoon. Add the milk, a little at a time, continuing to stir to avoid lumps.

- Switch now to a balloon whisk. Continue to stir over a medium heat until the sauce begins to thicken. The balloon whisk will also help eradicate any lumps that may have formed. Add more milk as necessary to get the desired thickness. The sauce should be the thickness of custard. Add the mustard and season with black pepper.

- Spoon a layer of bolognese mix into the bottom of your lasagne dish (make sure it fits into your halogen) and then pour over a thin layer of white sauce, followed by a layer of lasagne sheets.

● **Poultry**

Continue alternating the layers, finishing with the white sauce. Don't overfill the dish as the lasagne may spill out during cooking. Sprinkle grated cheese over the sauce.

- Place in the halogen on the low rack and cook at 200°C for 40–50 minutes, until golden and the lasagne sheets are cooked. If the top starts to get too dark, cover with tin foil, making sure it is secure. (The cooking time can be greatly reduced if you use fresh lasagne sheets.)

- Serve with salad and garlic bread.

Top Tip: Lasagnes work really well in the halogen oven but if you want to speed up the whole process, use fresh lasagne sheets. This will cut the cooking time down by half and avoid a dark top. If you don't want to go to the expense of fresh pasta sheets (and don't want to make your own), you can boil the pasta sheets for 5 minutes before placing them in your lasagne dish. This gives them a head start and can shorten overall cooking time.

If you fancy garlic bread with your lasagne, you can add this to the halogen 5–10 minutes before the end of the cooking time. If there is room you can place the garlic bread on the shelf with the lasagne dish. If there is limited room, transfer your lasagne to the base of the halogen and place a rack above the lasagne dish. Pop the garlic bread onto this.

Serves 4

Chicken Arrabiata

Ingredients:
Chilli oil
1 onion, sliced
2 red peppers, sliced
1 red chilli, sliced
2–3 cloves garlic, roughly
 chopped
3–4 chicken fillets, diced
1 jar pasta sauce (ideally chilli
 and tomato)
1 tin chopped tomatoes

You can make this dish with pasta or it is just as nice with some crusty bread for a quick and easy supper. I use a stainless steel dish that is hob proof and ovenproof. If you don't have one, you will need to transfer from the sauté pan into an ovenproof dish.

- Add a little chilli oil to your sauté pan and place over a medium heat. Add the onion, peppers, chilli, garlic and chicken and cook until the chicken starts to turn white on both sides.

- Add the pasta sauce and chopped tomatoes and cook for another 5 minutes.

- Place this in the halogen oven on the low rack (either in your sauté pan if possible or transfer to an ovenproof dish). Set the temperature to 180°C and cook for 15–20 minutes.

- Serve with pasta or crusty bread.

● **Poultry**

Serves 4

Preparation time:
10 minutes
Cooking time:
20-25 minutes

Chicken, Goat's Cheese, Red Pepper and Cherry Tomato Bake

Goat's cheese works perfectly with peppers and tomatoes. This is one of my favourite dishes.

Ingredients:
4 chicken breasts
110g goat's cheese
Black pepper
1 punnet cherry tomatoes, halved
2 red peppers, thickly sliced
2 red onions, cut into wedges
Olive oil
Balsamic vinegar
Sea salt
Sugar

- Wash your chicken breasts. Using a very sharp knife, slit a hole in one side of each breast to form a pocket. Fill with the goat's cheese.

- Place the chicken breasts in an ovenproof dish (making sure it fits in your halogen oven). Season to taste with black pepper.

- Place the cherry tomatoes, peppers and red onion around the chicken breasts. Drizzle the vegetables with olive oil and balsamic vinegar and finish with a sprinkle of sea salt and sugar.

- Place in the halogen on the high rack and bake at 200°C for 20–25 minutes until golden.

- Serve with a lovely green salad.

Preparation time:
10 minutes

Cooking time:
40 minutes

Serves 4

Pan-roasted Vegetables and Chicken Breasts Wrapped in Parma Ham

Ingredients:
350g new potatoes, washed
    and halved
2 red onions, cut into wedges
3–4 cloves garlic, whole
1 red pepper, cut into wedges
12 cherry tomatoes
Olive oil
2–3 sprigs thyme
4 chicken breasts
4–6 slices Parma ham
Paprika
Seasoning to taste

This one-pot dish needs no accompaniments, other than perhaps a green salad. You can use potato wedges in this recipe but I find new potatoes are best. Leave them whole unless they are too large – you really want them all around the same size otherwise they will cook unevenly.

- Place the vegetables in an oiled ovenproof dish or roasting tin, making sure it fits well in your halogen oven. Drizzle with oil and add the sprigs of thyme. Toss well to ensure everything is evenly coated.

- Place in the halogen on the high rack, set the temperature to 220°C and cook for 10 minutes.

- Meanwhile, wrap the chicken breasts in the Parma ham.

- Remove the lid of the halogen and carefully (don't burn yourself) make a gap in the vegetables. Then place the chicken breasts, Parma ham seam down, into the dish. Sprinkle the chicken with paprika. Season to taste.

- Place the lid back on, lower the temperature to 200°C and cook for 20–30 minutes, or until the chicken is cooked to your specification. If the vegetables start to brown too much, you can cover with foil, but the tomatoes and peppers go very sweet when they start to darken and this can add to the flavour.

- Serve when the chicken is cooked to your satisfaction.

- **Poultry**

Serves 4–6

Preparation time:
10 minutes
Cooking time:
40 minutes

Simple Chicken, Mushroom and Bacon Filo Pie

This is a very simple dish which looks far more impressive than it really is. Cook it in advance for an effortless meal.

- In a sauté pan, heat the olive oil over a medium heat. Add the chicken pieces and cook until they start to brown. Add the bacon, onion and mushroom and continue to cook for another 5 minutes.

- Add the cream cheese and milk, and stir well until it forms a creamy sauce. If you like a really creamy taste, you could add a dollop or two of crème fraîche or natural Greek yoghurt.

- Add the thyme and season before removing from the heat. Pour the mixture into a deep pie dish. I use a deep-sided ovenproof dish.

- Melt the butter in a saucepan. Cut the filo pastry sheets in half. Brush each sheet very roughly with the melted butter. Scrunch up roughly/loosely and place randomly on the top of the chicken mixture. Continue until it is covered. Don't overload the top with tightly packed bundles of pastry, just make sure it is covered. Finish with a sprinkle of sesame seeds and a dash of black pepper.

- Place the pie in the halogen on the high rack and cook at 210°C for 20–30 minutes until golden and bubbly.

- Serve with mashed potato and seasonal vegetables.

Ingredients:
Olive oil
400g boneless chicken pieces, diced
8 rashers lean bacon, diced
1 red onion, diced
175g button mushrooms, halved
1 × 350g tub cream cheese
200ml milk
Crème fraîche or natural Greek yoghurt (optional)
2–3 sprigs thyme, finely chopped
Seasoning to taste
30g butter, melted
½ pack filo pastry
15g sesame seeds

Serves 4

Chicken, Mushroom and Bacon Lasagne

Ingredients:
Olive oil
200g mushrooms, sliced (a
    mixture of types is good)
8 rashers lean bacon, diced
Knob of butter
1 tablespoon plain flour or
    cornflour
350ml milk
250g cooked chicken,
    chopped
Black pepper
Sea salt
2 × 400g tins chopped
    tomatoes or 1 × large jar
    pasta/bolognese sauce
1 teaspoon dried mixed herbs
Lasagne sheets
250ml Greek yoghurt
1 beaten egg
1–2 tablespoons grated
    Parmesan cheese

This dish is ideal for using up any cooked chicken. As with all lasagnes cooked in the halogen, you can speed up the cooking process by using fresh lasagne sheets or parboil before adding to the dish.

- Place a little olive oil into a sauté pan and over a medium heat cook the mushrooms and bacon for 5–8 minutes. Remove from the heat.

- Melt the butter in a heavy-based saucepan. Add the flour and stir well with a wooden spoon. Gradually add the milk and bring slowly to the boil, stirring all the time. You may want to add more milk if you think it is too little.

- Add the chicken, mushrooms and bacon to the sauce. Stir well before seasoning with black pepper and sea salt.

- In another bowl, combine the tomatoes, herbs and seasoning together.

- Start to layer your lasagne by placing some of the tomato mixture in the base of a dish, followed by the lasagne sheets, followed by the chicken mixture. Continue, finishing with a layer of the lasagne sheets on the top.

- Mix together the yoghurt and the egg and spread over the lasagne. Sprinkle with the Parmesan cheese and season with black pepper.

- Place the lasagne in the halogen on the high rack. Set the temperature to 200°C and cook for approximately 40 minutes (you

- **Poultry**

can reduce the cooking time if you have parboiled the lasagne sheets or used fresh). If it starts to darken on top, cover securely with tin foil.

- Serve with potato wedges and green salad.

> **Top Tip**: My mum always taught me to make the most of the oven when cooking. The halogen oven is too small to cook several things at once but you can still save time by doubling up the recipe and freezing it uncooked ready to be defrosted and cooked at a later date. Remember to label the food and pop on a date. It is a great feeling to have a freezer full of home-cooked food ready for those days when you are too busy to spend much time in the kitchen.

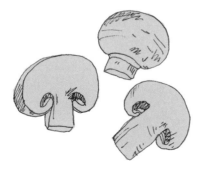

CHAPTER 3

Meat

The Halogen oven can cook meat slightly quicker than the conventional oven, though you have to be careful to get your temperature settings right. Too high and the tops of the joints or bird will burn whilst the middle may remain raw or undercooked. I would advise using a temperature gauge to test your meat, particularly poultry or joints of meat until you are more confident – even when following a recipe.

When meat is placed on the lower rack, it allows the juices and fats to drain away – therefore making the meat healthier. Some people worry that the meat will dry out too much, but to be honest, meat does tend to be very tender and moist when cooked in the Halogen Oven – unless you overcook it! If you are concerned, you can always place your meat on a baking tray or even cook on the base of the halogen cooker – ideal if you also want to add roast potatoes.

If you are cooking a joint you can cook as you would do in a conventional oven – roughly 20 minutes per 500g at 180°C and add another 10 minutes to the end of the cooking time.

As with all foods cooked in the Halogen Oven, make sure there is adequate space between the element and the food – ideally at least 2–3cm. The nearer the food is to the element, the more likely it is to burn or cook quickly. If you are concerned, wrap some foil over the food for the first half of the cooking, though make sure this is secured well as the power of the fan could lift this.

Serves 4

Preparation time:
10 minutes
Cooking time:
45 minutes

Sausage, Chorizo and Paprika One Pot

I used to love sausage and beans when I was little – this is a very grown-up version. Sometimes I like to heat things up a little by adding a couple of chopped chillies along with the onions and peppers.

Ingredients:
6–8 lean sausages
100g chorizo, cut into thick chunks
Olive oil
2 red onions, finely chopped
3–4 cloves garlic, roughly chopped
2 red peppers, sliced
1 dessertspoon runny honey
1 tin chopped tomatoes
1 tin baked beans
2 tablespoon smoked paprika
Seasoning to taste
2 handfuls of baby leaf spinach

- Place the sausages and chorizo on a browning tray and place in the halogen on the high rack. Drizzle with a small amount of olive oil. Cook at 220°C for 10 minutes and then add the onion, garlic and peppers. Continue to cook until browned, turning occasionally. You may want to drain off any fat at the end of the cooking time.

- Remove from the oven and place the sausages/onions in a casserole dish (make sure this fits well in your oven). Add the remaining ingredients apart from the spinach. Rinse out the tins of the tomatoes and baked beans with a little water (about one-third of each tin) and add this to the mixture. Combine well.

- Pop on a lid or secure a double layer of foil over the top before placing in the halogen on the low rack.

- Turn the temperature down to 200°C and cook for 25 minutes.

- Remove the lid and stir in the spinach leaves. Add more water if you think it needs it.

- Cook without a lid for another 10 minutes before serving with mash or crusty bread. Delicious!

Serves 4

Healthy Lamb Biryani

Ingredients:
Olive oil spray
450g lean lamb, cubed (if you
    are really health conscious,
    you could swap lamb for
    Quorn)
1 red onion, diced
2 cloves garlic, crushed
1 teaspoon ground cinnamon
1 teaspoon ground cardamom
½ teaspoon ground cloves
2–3 teaspoon curry powder
1 chilli, chopped (optional)
350ml plain 0% fat Greek
    yoghurt
150ml lamb stock
4 tomatoes, diced
250g brown basmati rice
Toasted almonds to sprinkle

Forget takeaways – make your own healthier and tastier versions of your favourite dishes. You can make the lamb mixture in advance and just cook the rice when you are ready to assemble.

- In a sauté pan over a medium/high heat, add a spray of oil and heat until hot. Add the lamb, onion and garlic and cook until the lamb starts to brown and the onion starts to soften.

- Add the spices and cook for a couple of minutes before adding the yoghurt, stock and tomatoes. Combine well and gently cook on a low heat for 10 minutes.

- Meanwhile, cook your rice as directed by the manufacturer. I normally add 1 ½ water to rice, bring to the boil and leave simmering for a couple of minutes before popping a lid on and removing completely from heat. Leave to stand for 10–12 minutes. Fluff up using a fork.

- Place a layer of rice in the bottom of your ovenproof dish (make sure your dish fits in your halogen!). Follow this with a layer of the lamb mixture. Continue layering until you have used up all the ingredients. Pour over 150ml water.

- Cover with foil and place in the halogen oven on the low rack. Cook at 180°C for 15–20 minutes.

- Garnish with toasted almonds before serving.

Serves 4–6

Roast Leg of Lamb with Roasted Vegetables

Preparation time:
15 minutes
Cooking time:
1 hour, 20 minutes

Perfect for Sunday roast.

- Mix together the garlic, chilli, rosemary, seasoning and olive oil to form a paste. Rub this over the leg of lamb. You can score the flesh first to help give the paste something to hold on to. Place in the halogen on the low rack, set to 230°C and cook for 15 minutes.

- Meanwhile, cut the potatoes into size and steam or parboil for 10 minutes. Drain and return to an empty saucepan. Add the paprika and semolina. Pop the lid back on the saucepan and shake to fluff up and coat the vegetables.

- Place the potatoes around the lamb. Brush or spray with olive oil. Halve the onions and place with the potatoes, along with the sprigs of rosemary. Remember to turn the lamb and vegetables regularly during cooking and add a brush or spray of oil or paste as required.

- Cook for another 10 minutes before reducing the temperature to 180°C and cooking for another 30–45 minutes or until both the meat and potatoes are cooked to your satisfaction. Cooking times for lamb depend on the size of the joint.

Ingredients:
1 leg of lamb
3–4 cloves garlic, crushed
½ teaspoon chopped chillies
1 teaspoon dried rosemary
Seasoning
2–3 tablespoons olive oil
2 sweet potatoes
6–8 potatoes
2 red onions
2–3 teaspoons paprika
2–3 teaspoons semolina
2–3 tablespoons olive oil
2–3 sprigs rosemary

Serves 4

Sausage and Bean Bonanza

Ingredients:
6–8 good quality sausages
2 red onions, cut into wedges
Olive oil
1 red pepper, thickly sliced
4 tomatoes, quartered
2 tins baked beans
2 teaspoons paprika
Black pepper

This makes a fantastic brunch or filling supper.

- Place the sausages and onion in a roasting dish. Drizzle with a very small amount of oil (the sausages will leak fat so you won't need much).

- Place in the halogen on the high rack and set the temperature to 200°C. Cook for 15 minutes, turning the sausages halfway through.

- Remove from the oven and drain any fat. Cut the sausages into large chunks and leave in the roasting tray with the onion. Add the pepper and tomatoes.

- Place back in the oven for another 10 minutes.

- Remove and add the baked beans, paprika, 200ml water and season with black pepper.

- Place back in the oven and cook for another 10 minutes until bubbling.

- Serve immediately with chunky bread or as a delicious topping for jacket potatoes.

● **Meat**

Serves 4

Preparation time:
10–15 minutes
Cooking time:
25 minutes

Lamb and Vegetable One-pot Roast

The sweet potatoes, carrots, tomatoes and red onions are nutrient rich, making this dish great for your health.

Ingredients:
Olive oil
6–8 lamb chops
500g new potatoes
2 sweet potatoes, cut into
  thick chunks
1 large carrot, cut into thick
  chunks
2 red onions, cut into wedges
3 cloves garlic, roughly
  chopped
2–3 sprigs thyme
Sea salt
Black pepper
200g cherry tomatoes
Balsamic vinegar

- Drizzle your roasting dish with olive oil and add the lamb chops.

- In a bowl, add the vegetables (apart from the tomatoes), the garlic, thyme and a drizzle of olive oil. Combine well.

- Pour this into the roasting dish, moving the chops so everything is evenly distributed. Season to taste.

- Place the dish in the halogen on the low rack and cook at 190°C for 15 minutes.

- Remove and add the cherry tomatoes. Drizzle with balsamic and a little more oil if needed. Place back in the oven and cook for another 5–10 minutes at 210°C.

- Serve immediately.

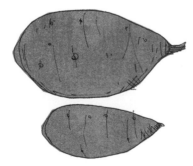

Preparation time:
10 minutes

Cooking time:
25 minutes

Chorizo and Tomato Soup

Ingredients:
100g chorizo, sliced
1 large red onion, diced
1 red pepper, diced
3 cloves garlic, diced
Drizzle of olive oil
1 tin chopped tomatoes
2 fresh tomatoes, finely
    chopped
1 teaspoon sundried tomato
    paste
Handful of fresh basil leaves
400ml vegetable stock
Black pepper
Sea salt

A lovely tomato soup with a kick of paprika.

- Place the chorizo, onion, pepper and garlic in an ovenproof dish. Drizzle with a small amount of olive oil – you don't need much as the chorizo will leak lots of oil.

- Place in the halogen on the high rack and set the temperature to 200°C. Cook for 5 minutes, then turn and cook for another 5 minutes.

- Remove from the heat carefully. Add the remaining ingredients and season to taste. Cover with a lid or double layer of foil, held securely.

- Place back in the oven at the same temperature and cook for another 20 minutes.

- Stir well before serving with crusty bread.

- Meat

Lamb Hotpot

Preparation time:
10 minutes
Cooking time:
1 hour, 30 minutes

Traditionally a Lancashire hotpot (made with lamb or mutton) would be cooked slowly all day to produce succulent meat. If you opt for tougher cuts, they will benefit from slow cooking, but those who want quicker and easier meals can speak to their butchers for advice about the best cut.

Ingredients:
400g lamb, cubed
50g plain flour
2–3 teaspoons paprika
Olive oil
3–4 leeks, sliced
2 cloves garlic, crushed
1–2 carrots, chopped
Knob of butter
500ml lamb stock
1 teaspoon mixed herbs
2–3 sprigs thyme (or cube of frozen fresh thyme)
4 large potatoes, thinly sliced
25g mature Cheddar, grated

- In a bowl, mix the lamb with the flour and paprika, ensuring the lamb is evenly coated all over.

- Heat a little olive oil in a large sauté pan and fry the leeks and garlic for 2–3 minutes. Add the meat, carrots and butter and cook for a further 2–3 minutes to help brown the meat.

- Pour on the stock, dried herbs and thyme and cook for 10 minutes.

- Place a layer of potato slices in the bottom of a greased casserole dish (make sure it fits in the halogen). Cover with a layer of meat mixture and continue alternating layers of meat and potato, finishing with a final layer of potato slices. Pop on a lid or cover securely with tin foil.

- Turn on the halogen to 210°C. Place the casserole dish on the low rack and cook for 45 minutes.

- Remove from the oven and sprinkle over the grated cheese before returning the hotpot to the oven without a lid for a final 20–25 minutes until the potatoes are tender.

Serves 4

Bacon, Chorizo and Potato Hash

Ingredients:
3–4 large potatoes, cut into
   2–3cm chunks
Olive oil
100g chorizo, cut into thick
   slices
1 pack lean thick bacon, cut
   into thick chunks
1 large onion, chopped
Paprika
Black pepper
Sea salt

Chorizo is traditionally a pork sausage made with smoked paprika. It gives off a lovely vibrant red colour to dishes and leaves a delicious paprika flavour. The skin can sometimes be a problem as it is tough so you may want to remove it.

- Boil or steam the potato chunks until they are just starting to soften – don't overcook!

- Drain the potatoes and place in an oiled baking tray. Add the chorizo, bacon and chopped onion. Sprinkle with paprika and season with black pepper and sea salt. Drizzle with a little olive oil.

- Set your halogen to 210°C. Place on the high rack and cook for 20–30 minutes, or until the chorizo, bacon and potatoes are cooked and crispy. It may help to toss the contents halfway through the cooking time, to ensure everything is evenly cooked and crisp.

- Serve immediately for a tasty supper or brunch.

Serves 4

Pan-roasted Breakfast

Preparation time:
10 minutes
Cooking time:
25 minutes

Don't think this is only suitable for breakfast, it's ideal for a lovely supper, especially when you require comfort food.

- Place the tomatoes, garlic and bacon in an ovenproof dish (making sure it fits in your halogen). Sprinkle with olive oil, sea salt and black pepper.

- Place in the halogen on the high rack at 200°C for 10 minutes.

- Remove from the oven. Make 4 spaces evenly in the mixture and crack an egg into each space.

- Cover the dish with a lid or securely held foil and bake for a further 10–15 minutes until the eggs are cooked to your taste.

- Remove from the oven, sprinkle with parsley and serve immediately with warm crusty bread.

Ingredients:
2 punnets cherry tomatoes
3 cloves garlic
1 pack thick bacon, roughly
    chopped
Olive oil
Sea salt
Black pepper
4 large eggs
2 tablespoons parsley,
    chopped

Serves 4

Moussaka

Ingredients:
2–3 aubergines, sliced
Olive oil
1 onion, finely chopped
2 cloves garlic, crushed
400g lamb mince
1 tin chopped tomatoes
2 teaspoons tomato purée
1 teaspoon dried mint
2 teaspoons ground cinnamon
Seasoning to taste
300ml low-fat crème fraîche
50g mature Cheddar or
    Parmesan cheese, grated

A family favourite in our home. Friends of mine don't like aubergines so they use very thinly sliced potato instead. Both are delicious.

- Place the aubergines in a pan of boiling water for 2 minutes. Remove and pat dry. Leave to one side.

- Meanwhile, heat a little olive oil in a sauté pan and fry the onion and garlic. Add the lamb mince and cook until brown.

- Add the tomatoes, tomato purée, mint, cinnamon and seasoning and cook for another 2–3 minutes.

- Select your ovenproof dish – I normally use a Pyrex or lasagne dish for this – making sure it fits into your halogen oven. Place a layer of mince into the dish, followed by a layer of aubergine. Continue alternating mince and aubergine, finishing with a layer of mince.

- Mix the crème fraîche with the grated cheese and pour over the final layer of mince. Garnish with a sprinkle of Parmesan.

- Place in the halogen on the low rack and cook at 210°C for 30–35 minutes until bubbling.

● **Meat**

Serves 4

Chorizo, Leek and Butterbean Hotpot

Preparation time:
10 minutes
Cooking time:
35 minutes

This is a good dish for using up any leftover cooked potatoes.

- If you don't have any leftover cooked potatoes, cook them now while you prepare the rest of the dish.

- Place the chorizo, garlic, spring onions and leeks in an ovenproof dish. Drizzle with a little olive oil and dot with butter.

- Place in the halogen on the high rack and cook for 5 minutes at 220°C. Then turn and cook for another 5 minutes.

- Remove from the oven. Mix the cornflour with a little water (about 30–40ml) and stir well. Pour this into the dish and stir, making sure you pick up any browned bits in the dish.

- Add the butter beans, wine or vermouth and stock. Season to taste.

- Place the potatoes over the top, making sure they are overlapping each other to cover the entire surface.

- Cover with the grated cheese and season again with black pepper.

- Place back in the oven but this time on the low rack. Reduce the temperature to 180°C and cook for 20 minutes until hot and bubbling and the potatoes are golden.

- Serve immediately with a lovely salad.

Ingredients:
4–5 potatoes, cooked and
  thickly sliced
100g chorizo, roughly
  chopped
3 cloves garlic, roughly
  crushed
4 spring onions, finely
  chopped
2 leeks, finely chopped
Olive oil
25g butter
1 tablespoon cornflour
2 tins butterbeans, drained
200ml white wine or
  vermouth
350ml vegetable stock
Black pepper
50g mature Cheddar cheese,
  grated

Preparation time:
10 minutes

Cooking time:
45 minutes

Serves 4

Toad in the Hole

Ingredients:
100g plain flour
300ml milk
1 egg
1 onion, chopped
8 lean sausages
Olive oil
Handful of fresh herbs such
    as thyme, oregano,
    rosemary, or 2 teaspoons
    dried herbs
Seasoning to taste

A family favourite, perfect with red onion gravy and mash!

- Using a mixer with a balloon whisk, blend the flour, milk and egg together to form a batter. Mix thoroughly and leave to settle.

- Meanwhile place the onion, sausages and a drizzle of olive oil in a deep ovenproof dish that fits well in your halogen oven. Place on the high rack and cook at 200°C for 8–10 minutes, turning occasionally.

- Just before the 10 minutes are up, give the batter mix a quick whizz with your balloon whisk, adding the herbs and seasoning before another final whizz.

- Remove the sausages from the oven and immediately pour over the batter, ensuring that all the sausages are covered.

- Return to the oven and cook on the low rack for 30–35 minutes until golden.

- Serve with red onion gravy and steamed vegetables or mash.

- Meat

Serves 4

Pork, Apple and Cider One Pot

Preparation time:
10 minutes
Cooking time:
40–45 minutes

Pork and apple – they go together so well.

- Place the pork in an ovenproof dish, drizzle with olive oil and place on the high rack of your halogen.

- Set the temperature to 200°C and cook for 5–8 minutes, turning/stirring occasionally during cooking to ensure it is evenly browned.

- Remove from the oven. Place the pork on a dish and add the onion to the ovenproof dish. Add a little more oil if needed and cook at the same temperature for 5 minutes to allow it to soften.

- Add the apple and cook for another 5 minutes, before adding the pork. Cook for another 3 minutes.

- Add all the remaining ingredients and combine well. Add a lid or double layer of tin foil, held securely.

- Place back in the halogen and cook at 180°C for 20 minutes.

Ingredients:
500g pork, thickly diced
Olive oil
1 large red onion, diced
2 apples, cored, peeled and cut into wedges
250ml cider
200ml chicken or vegetable stock
2–3 tablespoons crème fraîche
1 tablespoon wholegrain mustard
Black pepper

Ingredients:
4 leeks
25g butter
1 tablespoon plain flour or
    cornflour
500–750ml milk
2 tablespoons nutritional
    yeast flakes (optional)
75g mature cheese
½ teaspoon mustard
Black pepper to taste
8 slices lean ham or bacon
2–3 tablespoons
    home-prepared wholemeal
    breadcrumbs
2 tablespoons oats
25g Parmesan cheese

Serves 4

Ham and Leek Cheesy Bake

When you are seeking comfort food, this really does hit the mark.

- Trim the leeks top and tail to about 10–12.5cm in lengths and steam for 5–8 minutes until tender.

- Meanwhile, melt the butter gently in a saucepan on a medium heat (not high!). Add the flour or cornflour and stir well with a wooden spoon. Add the milk, a little at a time, continuing to stir to avoid lumps.

- Switch to a balloon whisk and continue to stir over a medium heat until the sauce begins to thicken. The balloon whisk will also help eradicate any lumps that may have materialised. Add more milk as necessary to get the desired thickness. The sauce should be the thickness of custard.

- If you are using nutritional yeast flakes, add these first as they will reduce the amount of cheese you may need – taste as you go! Then add the cheese and mustard, and stir well. Season with black pepper.

- Remove the leeks from the steamer and wrap a slice of ham or bacon around each one. Lay them in the base of an ovenproof dish – lasagne dishes are good for this but make sure it fits well in your halogen oven.

- Pour over the cheese sauce.

- **Meat**

- Combine the breadcrumbs, oats and Parmesan cheese and sprinkle over the leek and cheese bake.

- Place in the halogen on the low rack and cook at 220°C for 15 minutes until golden and bubbnling.

Top Tip: If you are watching your weight or want to cut down on high fats, you can swap milk for soya or skimmed milk, change the cheese to low fat mature cheddar and add some seeds to the crumbly topping (as this gives you extra omega 3 and protein). Nutritional yeast flakes are suitable for vegans. Adding this to a sauce gives you a cheesy flavour which means you need less cheese to create a good taste. Add wholegrain mustard to add more flavour.

Serves 4

Lasagne

Ingredients:
1 onion, finely chopped
2–3 cloves garlic, finely
  chopped
A spray of olive oil
1 pepper, finely chopped
  (optional)
400g lean beef mince or, for
  vegetarians, veggie mince
150ml red wine
75g mushrooms, finely
  chopped (optional)
3–4 fresh tomatoes, chopped,
  or 1 tin chopped tomatoes
Mixed herbs to taste
Seasoning to taste

For the white sauce
25g butter
1 tablespoon plain flour or
  cornflour
500–750ml milk
¼ teaspoon mustard
  (optional)
Black pepper to taste

Lasagne sheets (ensure the
  pack says 'no precooking
  required')
Grated cheese to garnish

This is my son's favourite – though, like most children, he prefers it without mushrooms (though I do cheat and cut them small so he doesn't notice!).

- Fry the onion and garlic in a little olive oil until soft and translucent. Add the pepper if you are using one.

- Add the mince and cook until brown, followed by the wine and mushrooms if you are including them, and cook for 2 more minutes.

- Add the fresh or tinned tomatoes (or 'cheat' pasta sauce), stirring well. Finally, add the herbs and season to taste. Leave to simmer for 5 minutes.

- While the bolognese mix is simmering, make the white sauce. Melt the butter gently in a saucepan on a medium heat (not high!). Add the flour or cornflour and stir well with a wooden spoon. Add the milk, a little at a time, continuing to stir to avoid lumps.

- Switch now to a balloon whisk. Continue to stir over a medium heat until the sauce begins to thicken. The balloon whisk will also help eradicate any lumps that may have formed. Add more milk as necessary to get the desired thickness. The sauce should be the thickness of custard. Add the mustard and season with black pepper.

- Spoon a layer of bolognese mix into the bottom of your lasagne dish (make sure it fits into your halogen), and then pour over a thin layer of white sauce, followed by a layer of lasagne sheets.

- **Meat**

Continue alternating the layers, finishing with the white sauce. Don't overfill the dish as the lasagne may spill out during cooking.

- Sprinkle grated cheese over the sauce.

- Place on the low rack in the halogen oven and cook at 200°C for 40–50 minutes, until golden and the lasagne sheets are cooked. If the top starts to get too dark, cover with tin foil, making sure it is secure. (The cooking time can be greatly reduced if you use fresh lasagne sheets.)

- Serve with salad and garlic bread.

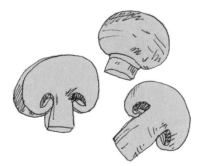

Preparation time:
10–15 minutes

Cooking time:
45 minutes

Ingredients:
800g potatoes, cut into rough
  chunks
4 carrots, 2 roughly chopped,
  2 cut into small cubes
A spray of olive oil
1 onion, chopped
400g lean mince (or
  pre-drained of fat)
75g mushrooms, sliced
  (optional)
100ml red wine
1 teaspoon yeast extract
  (Marmite or similar)
200ml meat stock or
  vegetable stock if using
  veggie mince, heated
Seasoning to taste
Worcestershire sauce
25g butter
75g mature Cheddar
Paprika for sprinkling

Serves 4–6

Shepherd's and Cottage Pie

The only real difference between shepherd's pie and cottage pie is the meat. Shepherd's pie traditionally is made with lamb mince and cottage pie with beef. Nowadays you can make these dishes using a variety of minced meat or vegetarian mince if you prefer.

- Place the potatoes and the 2 chopped carrots in a steamer and cook until soft.

- Meanwhile, heat the oil in a large sauté pan and fry the onion for 1–2 minutes before adding the mince.

- Cook until brown before adding the 2 cubed carrots, the mushrooms and the wine.

- Dissolve the yeast extract in the hot stock before adding to the mince.

- Cook for 15 minutes until tender and reduced to the desired consistency. Season to taste and add a few splashes of Worcestershire sauce.

- Mash the steamed potato and carrots together. Add the butter and two-thirds of the Cheddar. Mix thoroughly.

- Place the mince in a deep ovenproof dish and spoon the mash over the top. Be careful not to overfill the dish. Press the mash down gently with a fork. Top with the remaining grated cheese and a sprinkle of paprika.

- Place in the halogen on the low rack and cook at 200°C for 20–25 minutes.

- **Meat**

Serves 4

Beef and Vegetable Cobbler

Preparation time:
15 minutes
Cooking time:
1 hour

This is a very filling meal – you really don't need to serve it with anything else.

- Place the beef steak in a bowl and coat with the flour and paprika.

- Heat a little olive oil in an ovenproof casserole dish and place on your hob. If dish is not hob proof, use a sauté pan and then transfer. Remember to make sure it fits comfortably in your halogen oven as it will need to be transferred at a later stage. Add the onion, leeks, carrot and celery and cook for 2 minutes.

- Add the redcurrant jelly and stir well. Gradually add the wine, beef stock and button mushrooms. Add the dried herbs if using; if you're using fresh, add half now and half before you add the scones. Cook for another 5 minutes to keep the temperature up.

- Remove from the hob, cover and place on the low rack of the halogen oven. Cover with a lid or double layer of foil, making sure this is secure. Cook at 180°C for 30 minutes.

- Meanwhile, place the flour in a bowl. Add the yoghurt, oil and chopped parsley. Mix to form a soft dough. Place on a floured board and shape into individual balls. Flatten slightly.

- Remove the lid or foil from the casserole dish and stir the casserole. If you are using fresh herbs, add the remaining half. Add more beef stock if needed. Place the scones on the top of the casserole, forming a circle or completely covering the top. You should be able to do this without having to lift out the casserole, but be careful not to burn yourself.

- Continue to bake for another 20 minutes, until the scones are golden and fluffy. Serve immediately.

Ingredients:
450g beef stewing steak, cut
  into cubes
50g plain flour
3 teaspoons paprika
Olive oil
1 onion, finely chopped
2 leeks, sliced
1 large carrot, diced
3 sticks celery, diced
2 tablespoons redcurrant jelly
300ml red wine
400ml beef stock (extra stock
  may be necessary)
125g button mushrooms
Handful of fresh herbs or 1
  teaspoon mixed dried herbs

Cobble/scone mix
100g self-raising flour
75ml natural yoghurt
2 tablespoons olive oil
Small handful of parsley,
  chopped

Serves 4–6

Sweet Potato and Meatball Casserole

Ingredients:

Casserole
2 large onions, finely chopped
2–3 cloves garlic, roughly chopped
2 carrots, diced
2 sticks celery, diced
2 sweet potatoes, diced
1 tin chopped tomatoes
500ml vegetable stock (extra stock may be necessary)
1 tablespoon paprika
2 bay leaves
Seasoning to taste

Meatballs
400g beef mince
1 small onion, finely chopped or grated
1 teaspoon paprika
1 teaspoon cumin
1 chilli, finely chopped
1 teaspoon chilli powder
2 teaspoons Worcestershire sauce
1 teaspoon parsley, roughly chopped
50g breadcrumbs
1 egg, beaten
Seasoning to taste
Drizzle of olive oil

Chopped parsley to sprinkle

I love using sweet potatoes in dishes. This is a great recipe – if you make up a big batch of meatballs, you can freeze them to use later in dishes like this one or the more traditional meatball in rich tomato sauce served with spaghetti.

- Place all the ingredients for the casserole in an ovenproof casserole dish (making sure it fits well in the halogen oven) and season to taste. Add a lid (the casserole lid or a double layer of tin foil securely fitted) and place the dish on the high rack. If you are concerned about the lid touching the element on the halogen lid, either use an extension ring or cook on the lower rack. The benefit of the high rack is that it allows more air to circulate all the way around the dish.

- Cook at 210°C for 35–45 minutes.

- Meanwhile, combine all the meatball ingredients apart from the olive oil together in a bowl and mix thoroughly.

- Form the mixture into small balls and place on a baking sheet. Cover with cling film and place in the fridge for 20 minutes to rest.

- Fry your meatballs in a sauté pan using a small amount of olive oil, until they are golden brown.

- Remove the lid from the casserole and add the meatballs. Check the liquid in the casserole – you may want to add more stock if it has evaporated. Combine well before popping the lid back on and cooking again for another 15–20 minutes, making sure the potato and carrots are tender.

- Serve with a sprinkle of parsley.

Top Tip: You can freeze the meatballs raw. I normally place them, still on the baking tray, in the freezer until they are firm. Then I remove them from the tray and place in a freezer bag. This way they won't stick together and you can pull out the required number of meatballs as and when you need them.

Ingredients:
3 large potatoes, peeled and
    cut into 3 (at an angle to
    create roast potato sizes)
1 tablespoon semolina
½ tablespoon paprika
Olive oil or vegetable oil
4 good quality sausages
1 large red onion, cut into
    wedges
8-10 vine tomatoes
1-2 courgettes, cut into thick
    wedges

Serves 2

Sausage Pot Roast

This recipe serves 2 but if you want to double it up to serve 4 you will have to cook on two racks and use the extension ring as you may not fit it all into one dish.

- Boil or steam the potatoes until the edges just start to soften and fluff up when touched. This should take about 10 minutes.

- Drain the potatoes and place back in the saucepan without water. Add the semolina and paprika, pop on a lid and shake well to bash the potatoes slightly and to disperse the semolina and paprika.

- Meanwhile, place your roasting dish in the halogen and add 1–2cm of oil in the base (olive or vegetable oil is fine). Set the temperature to 230°C and heat for 5 minutes.

- Carefully remove the dish (the oil is very hot so be careful). Using tongs, drop the potatoes into the oil carefully so they don't splash. Once they are all in you can turn them gently ensuring they are covered in oil but the semolina/paprika is still holding. Add more paprika if you want a richer colour.

- Place the dish back in the oven on the high rack and cook for 25 minutes at 210°C.

- Meanwhile, you can prepare the vegetables.

- Remove the dish from the oven and **drain away any excess oil**. Turn the potatoes before adding the sausages and onion wedges, making sure they are evenly spaced and not on top of the potatoes.

- **Meat**

- Place back in the oven at the same temperature for another 10 minutes.

- Remove and add the tomatoes and courgettes, pushing them into any gaps in the roasting pan. Cook for another 15 minutes, by which time the roast potatoes and sausages should be cooked – cook for longer if you think it nneeds extra browning.

- Serve immediately.

Top Tip: Remember you can wash your halogen bowl using the wash setting on your halogen controls. Empty the bowl and fill no more than $1/3$ up the sides with hot water (check your manufacturers instructions to make sure you don't overfill your machine with water as this could damage the element). Add a squirt of washing liquid. Turn the setting to wash mode and set the timer for 5–10 minutes (depending on how dirty the bowl is). The liquid in the bowl will start to swish around, cleaning as it goes. I have known people use this setting as a mini dishwasher! Carefully remove the bowl when finished and tip the water away. The bowl is heavy and can be slippery when wet so take extra care. Wipe clean with a cloth. If you don't want to use this setting, you could place the bowl directly into your dishwasher.

Refer to your manufacturers instructions when cleaning the lids.

Serves 4

Lamb and Apricot Casserole

Ingredients:
A drizzle or spray of olive oil
1 onion, chopped
2–3 cloves garlic, crushed
400g lamb, diced
3 teaspoons harissa paste or
hot chilli paste
2 teaspoons ground cinnamon
300ml red wine
1 tin chopped tomatoes
400ml hot water or stock
1 tin chickpeas, drained
75g dried apricots, chopped
Fresh coriander leaves to
garnish
Sour cream to serve

This has a Moroccan feel to it – delicious.

- Heat the oil in a sauté or frying pan and cook the onion, garlic and lamb for 2–3 minutes. Add the harissa or hot chilli paste and stir well for 2 minutes.

- Place the lamb mixture in a casserole dish, making sure it fits comfortably in your halogen. Add all the remaining ingredients and combine well. Pop on the casserole lid or cover securely with tin foil. Place on the low rack and cook at 200°C for 50–60 minutes.

- Remove the lid and cook for another 5–10 minutes before serving garnished with coriander leaves and a side dish of sour cream.

- Meat

Serves 4

Sausage Casserole

Preparation time:
10 minutes
Cooking time:
40 minutes

My Aunty Mabel used to make us a similar dish on Bonfire night when we stayed on the farm. This is a really hearty dish, perfect for autumn evenings.

- Place the sausages, bacon and sliced onion on the grill pan. Drizzle with olive oil and cook on the high rack at 230°C until the sausages are browned and the onion softened.

- In a casserole dish (making sure this fits well in your halogen), put the sausages, onions, and all remaining ingredients. Season to taste.

- Pop a lid on the casserole dish, or make a lid using double-folded tin foil, securely fastened. Place in the halogen on the low rack and turn the temperature down to 200°C. Cook for 20–30 minutes until the vegetables are soft.

- Serve with mashed or jacket potatoes.

Ingredients:
1 pack lean, good quality sausages
4–6 rashers bacon or lardons, chopped
1 large red onion, sliced
Olive oil
2 cloves garlic, crushed
2 red peppers, finely sliced
1 large sweet potato, diced
1 tin chopped tomatoes
175ml red wine
2 teaspoons paprika
Small handful of parsley, chopped
Seasoning

Ingredients:
175g macaroni
2–3 leeks, finely chopped
6–8 rashers bacon, roughly
   chopped
Olive oil or butter
25g butter
1 tablespoon plain flour or
   cornflour
500–750ml milk
2 tablespoons nutritional
   yeast flakes (optional)
75g mature cheese
½ teaspoon mustard
Black pepper to taste
2–3 tablespoons
   home-prepared wholemeal
   breadcrumbs
2 tablespoons oats
25g Parmesan cheese

Serves 4

Bacon, Leek and Macaroni Cheese Bake

The perfect supper for hungry teenagers!

- Place the macaroni in boiling water and cook until tender. (The cooking time depends on the type of macaroni you use, so refer to the instructions on the packet.)

- While that is cooking, gently fry your leeks and bacon in a little olive oil or butter. Once cooked, leave to one side.

- Meanwhile, melt 25g butter gently in a saucepan on a medium heat (not high!). Add the flour or cornflour and stir well with a wooden spoon. Add the milk, a little at a time, continuing to stir to avoid lumps.

- Switch to a balloon whisk and continue to stir over a medium heat until the sauce begins to thicken. The balloon whisk will also help eradicate any lumps that may have materialised. Add more milk as necessary to get the desired thickness – the sauce should be the thickness of custard.

- If you are using nutritional yeast flakes, add these first as they will reduce the amount of cheese you may need – taste as you go! Then add the cheese and mustard, and stir well. Season with black pepper.

- Drain the macaroni and combine this with the bacon, leeks and cheese sauce. Season to taste and pour into an ovenproof dish (make sure this fits well in your halogen oven).

- **Meat**

- Combine the breadcrumbs, oats and Parmesan cheese and sprinkle over the bake.

- Place in the halogen on the low rack and cook at 220°C for 20 minutes until golden and bubbnling.

> **Top Tip**: Macaroni cheese can be quite thick which is not very appetising – it needs to be a light, fluid dish, not something you can slice! To avoid this make sure your sauce is not too thick before adding to the macaroni, especially if you are making this in advance as the longer it is left standing the thicker it can become. You can make this dish with skimmed milk. Soya milk can work well but be aware that it may separate a little.

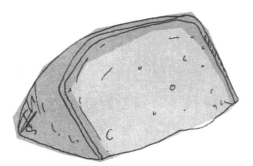

Ingredients:
6 slices stale bread, buttered
3–6 rashers bacon, diced or
    roughly chopped depending
    on preference
1 onion, finely chopped
150g mature Cheddar, grated
3 eggs
500ml milk
2 sprigs thyme, chopped
Seasoning to taste

Serves 4

Cheese, Bacon, Bread and Butter Savoury

This is a variation of the lovely and comforting bread and butter pudding.

- Grease an ovenproof dish, making sure it fits well into your halogen oven.

- Carefully line the ovenproof dish with buttered bread. Add the bacon, onion and cheese (leaving aside some cheese to top the bread later) between the layers and build up until you run out of bread. Alternatively, you could make bacon, onion and cheese sandwiches and line the dish with them, but I prefer the randomness.

- Beat the eggs and add the milk and thyme and season to taste. Pour this over the bread and leave to settle for about 20 minutes.

- Top the bread with some grated cheese and season with black pepper. Place in the halogen on the low rack and cook at 180°C for 30–40 minutes, until set.

Serves 4–6

Italian Beef Casserole

Preparation time:
10–15 minutes
Cooking time:
1 hour, 30 minutes

A very filling dish which is surprisingly simple to prepare.

- Place the flour and paprika in a bowl. Add the beef chunks and stir to evenly coat them in the flour.

- Place a little oil in a roasting tin and pop this into the halogen oven to heat on the high rack at 220°C.

- Once heated, add the beef, onion and garlic. Return to the high rack and cook for 5–10 minutes until browned and softened – you may have to stir a few times during cooking to ensure it is evenly browned.

- Remove from the oven and add the peppers, pancetta and cherry tomatoes. Cook again for another 5–8 minutes, stirring occasionally.

- Remove for the final time and add all the remaining ingredients but only half of the fresh herbs. Combine well and season to taste. Cover with a double layer of tin foil, making sure it is securely placed.

- Place the dish on the low rack and turn the heat down to 180°C. Cook for 1 hour. Remove the tin foil and add the remaining herbs. Cook again without the tin foil lid for another 15 minutes.

- Serve with jacket potatoes.

Ingredients:
1 tablespoon plain flour
3 teaspoons paprika
500g lean beef steak cut into chunks
Olive oil
2 red onions, cut into wedges
2–3 cloves garlic, finely chopped
2 red peppers, thickly sliced
200g pancetta, diced
300g cherry tomatoes
1 aubergine, diced
300ml red wine
400ml beef stock
2 tablespoons sundried tomato paste
100g olives
Small handful of fresh thyme and oregano combined
Seasoning

Preparation time:
5 minutes

Cooking time:
35 minutes

Pancetta and Three Cheese Bake

Ingredients:
140g plain flour
4 eggs, beaten
200ml milk
½ teaspoon oregano
Seasoning
1 red onion, very finely
  chopped
200g cubed pancetta
40g Gruyère cheese, grated
40g blue cheese, grated
30g Parmesan cheese, grated

A great dish for cheese lovers. This is one of those meals that makes you feel warm, cosy and satisfied.

- Combine the flour, eggs and milk until you have a smooth batter. Add the oregano and season to taste.

- Grease your ovenproof dish well.

- Mix the remaining ingredients with the batter and then pour this into your dish.

- Place in the halogen on the low rack and cook at 190°C for 25–35 minutes, until golden and firm to touch. It will puff up when cooked and flatten quite quickly, so serve immediately.

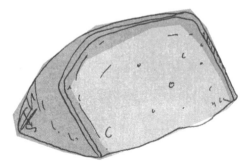

● **Meat**

Serves 4

Beef Cannelloni

Preparation time:
15 minutes

Cooking time:
1 hour, 10 minutes

I love cannelloni. I know it is the same as pasta sheets but somehow the cannelloni tubes just feel a little more special – though they are never that easy to fill without making a mess!

- Heat a little olive oil in a sauté pan, and sauté the beef and onion until browned. Add the chopped tomatoes, oregano and water or stock. Season to taste.

- Cook for 10–15 minutes, adding more water or stock if you need to.

- Meanwhile, combine the crème fraîche with the grated cheese, leaving a little cheese aside to place on the top of the dish. Add the milk, season and combine well.

- When the beef is ready, carefully fill the cannelloni tubes – this is a messy process, there is no way around this. Place them in neat rows in an ovenproof dish.

- Top with the crème fraîche mixture and scatter with the remaining grated cheese.

- Cover with a lid or double layer of foil, securely held. Place in the halogen on the low rack and cook for 45 minutes at 180°C. Remove the foil lid and cook for another 5–10 minutes to give the top a golden glow.

- Serve immediately with a green salad.

Ingredients:
Olive oil
400g lean beef mince
1 large onion, finely chopped
1 tin chopped tomatoes
1 teaspoon dried oregano
200ml water or beef stock
   (extra may be needed)
Black pepper
350g crème fraîche
125g mature Cheddar, grated
150ml milk
Cannelloni tubes

Serves 4

Pork Chops in Tomato and Pancetta Sauce

Ingredients:
4 pork chops
Olive oil
Black pepper
1 red onion, finely chopped
2 cloves garlic, crushed
100g diced pancetta
1 red pepper, sliced
1 tin chopped tomatoes
200ml red wine
Small handful fresh oregano,
    chopped

This rich tomato and pancetta sauce is perfect with pork chops.

- Place a little olive oil in a sauté pan and cook the chops over a medium heat for 3–4 minutes both sides.

- Remove and place in the base of an ovenproof dish, but keep the sauté pan on the medium heat.

- Place the onion, garlic, pancetta and pepper in the sauté pan and cook until the onion starts to soften and the pancetta browns.

- Add the tomatoes, wine and oregano. Cook for 5 minutes before pouring onto the chops.

- Cover with a lid or double layer of foil, securely held. Place in the halogen on the low rack and cook at 190°C for 20 minutes.

- Serve with green vegetables.

● **Meat**

Serves 4

Smoky Bacon and Bean Soup

Preparation time:
10 minutes
Cooking time:
45 minutes

This is a very filling soup. I love serving it with freshly baked bread rolls.

- Place some olive oil in a casserole dish (make sure it fits in your halogen). Add the onion, garlic and bacon.

- Place in the halogen on the high rack (if it will fit, if not the low rack is fine) and cook for 5 minutes at 250°C, turning and cooking for another few minutes until the onion is soft and the bacon starts to brown.

- Add all the remaining ingredients apart from the cabbage.

- Cover with a lid or double layer of foil, securely held. Place on the low rack and cook for 30 minutes at 210°C.

- Add the shredded cabbage and cook for another 10 minutes.

- Serve with crusty bread.

Ingredients:
Olive oil
1 red onion, finely chopped
2 cloves garlic, roughly chopped
4-6 rashers lean smoked bacon, diced
1 large carrot, diced
1 tin chopped tomatoes
2 teaspoons tomato purée (I prefer sundried tomato purée)
1 teaspoon paprika
1 bay leaf
450ml vegetable stock
2 tins mixed beans, drained
Seasoning to taste
50g cabbage, finely shredded

Serves 4

One-pot Italian Lamb Steaks

Ingredients:
1 tin tomatoes
200ml red wine
100g cherry tomatoes
1 large red onion, cut into
   thick slices or wedges
1 red pepper, cut into thick
   slices
3–5 cloves garlic, left whole
100g black olives, halved
3–4 sprigs thyme
Sea salt
Black pepper
4 lamb steaks

This is a really easy dish. You can prepare it in advance and leave in the fridge to marinate, or simply throw it together 30 minutes before you want to eat.

- In an ovenproof dish, add all the ingredients apart from the lamb, and combine until evenly coated and distributed. Place the lamb in amongst the vegetables and press down until just covered with the liquid. Place in the fridge, covered, until needed.

- When you are ready to cook, set the halogen to 210°C and place the dish on the high rack. Cook for 20–30 minutes until the lamb is cooked to your satisfaction.

- Serve immediately with crusty bread and a green salad.

Serves 4

Spicy Lamb Kofta

Preparation time:
10 minutes
Cooking time:
30 minutes

This is spicy meatballs in a curry sauce – so lovely yet quite simple. You could double up the meatball mixture and freeze some – a great way to save time when you fancy this dish again. My son loves to eat the warm meatballs in wraps or pitta bread.

- In a bowl, add all of the ingredients apart from the olive oil, half of the coriander leaves and the curry sauce. Combine well. Leave to rest for at least 2 hours.

- Scoop out small handfuls of the mixture and form into balls. (You can freeze these at this point: simply place them on a baking tray, pop in the freezer and when frozen you can place them into labelled freezer bags.)

- When you are ready to cook, fry the meatballs in a little olive oil until they are brown and cooked through.

- Transfer into an ovenproof dish. Pour over the curry sauce (rinse the jar with about a ¼ water and add this to the sauce) and sprinkle with the remaining freshly chopped coriander, reserving a little to garnish.

- Place in the halogen on the high rack and set the temperature to 190°C. Cook for 20 minutes.

- Garnish with coriander. Serve with rice, mango chutney and naan bread.

Ingredients:
500g lean lamb mince
1 onion, finely chopped
1 chilli, finely chopped
2-3 cloves garlic, crushed
1 teaspoon cumin
1 teaspoon ground coriander
2 teaspoons sweet curry
  powder
2cm knuckle fresh ginger,
  finely chopped
3 tablespoons mango chutney
Olive oil
Small handful of fresh
  coriander leaves, chopped
1 jar curry sauce (I use rogan
  josh)

Ingredients:
2–4 courgettes
Seasoning to taste
Olive oil
1 onion, finely chopped
2 cloves garlic, crushed
½–1 chilli, finely crushed
1–2 teaspoons curry powder
1 teaspoon cumin
1 teaspoon dried mint
½ teaspoon ground cinnamon
250g minced lamb
½ tin chopped tomatoes
30g sultanas

Serves 4

Stuffed Spicy Lamb Courgettes

This is a great dish for using any bolognese left over from a previous meal. Instead of cooking the lamb following the recipe, simply add some spices or tomatoes and herbs to your leftover bolognese and use this to stuff the courgettes. If you don't fancy stuffed courgettes, why not stuff a tomato, butternut squash or marrow?

- Cut the courgettes in half lengthways. Using a teaspoon, gently scoop out the soft flesh, retaining this for later. You should be left with approximately 2–3mm of flesh around the edges of each courgette.

- Place the courgettes on a baking tray. Season and drizzle with a little olive oil. Place in the halogen on the high rack and cook at 180°C for 15 minutes.

- Meanwhile, in a large sauté pan over a medium heat, heat some olive oil, and then add the onion, garlic and chilli. Cook this for a few minutes to help soften before adding the herbs and spices, shortly followed by the lamb.

- When the lamb has browned, add the chopped tomatoes and sultanas. You may want to add a little water if it starts to dry out. Season to taste.

- When the courgettes have started to soften, remove the tray from the halogen. Carefully spoon the mince mixture into the courgettes.

- Place them back into the halogen and continue to cook for another 10–15 minutes.

- Serve immediately.

- **Meat**

Bacon and Egg Salad

Preparation time:
10 minutes
Cooking time:
10–15 minutes

A burst of flavours for a delicious and simple salad.

- Boil or steam the potatoes with a little of the fresh mint.

- Meanwhile, hard-boil the eggs.

- Place the bacon on the browning tray and place in the halogen on the grill rack (see the section on grilling in Chapter 1, 'How to use your halogen oven'). Cook at 250°C until the bacon is crispy – this should take around 5–7 minutes but timing depends on the height of your rack.

- Place the salad leaves, spring onions, cherry tomatoes and cucumber in a large serving dish. Add the remaining mint and the chives. Combine well.

- In a jug, mix the olive oil, vinegar and wholegrain mustard, combine well and season to taste. Add more vinegar or olive oil to suit your own palate.

- Drain the potatoes when cooked and place in the serving dish.

- Chop the bacon and add to the salad. Finally halve or quarter the hard-boiled, shelled eggs and place on the top of the salad.

- Add the salad dressing to taste.

Ingredients:
750g new potatoes
Small handful of fresh mint
  leaves
4–6 eggs
1 pack lean bacon
75g salad leaves
½ bunch of spring onions,
  finely chopped
12–16 cherry tomatoes,
  halved
½ cucumber, diced
Small handful of chives,
  freshly chopped
2 tablespoons olive oil
1 tablespoon white wine
  vinegar
1 teaspoon wholegrain
  mustard
Seasoning to taste

Serves 4

Pork Steak Pot Roast

Ingredients:

500g new potatoes, left
   whole or halved if large
   (they need to be of an even
   size)
2 red onions, cut into wedges
3 cloves garlic, roughly
   chopped
300ml chicken stock
1–2 teaspoons sundried
   tomato paste
2 red peppers, cut into thick
   slices
1–2 sweet potatoes, cut into
   thick slices or wedges
2 courgettes, cut into thick
   slices
100g cherry or vine tomatoes,
   left whole
4 pork steaks
2 sprigs rosemary

A simple pot roast. You can use ordinary tomato paste but sundried gives a much nicer flavour.

- Place the new potatoes, onion and garlic in an ovenproof dish. Mix the chicken stock with the sundried tomato paste and pour over the potatoes. Cover with a lid or double layer of foil, held securely.

- Place in the halogen on the low rack and cook at 200°C for 20 minutes.

- Remove from the oven. Add all the remaining ingredients to the dish and re-cover.

- Place back in the oven and cook for another 10 minutes. Then remove the lid and cook for another 10–15 minutes until the steaks are done.

- Serve with green vegetables.

● Meat

Fish

We should all eat more oily fish – packed with essential omega 3, it should be included in at least three meals a week. Choose from mackerel, trout, salmon, sardines, pilchards, herring. I have included recipes for cod but if you are concerned about using cod, you can opt for alternatives such as coley or pollock – speak to your fishmonger for more ideas.

Preparation time:
5–10 minutes

Cooking time:
30–40 minutes

Serves 4

Smoked Haddock Chowder

Ingredients:
1 large onion, diced
4–6 rashers thick lean bacon, diced
2 sweet potatoes, diced
Drizzle of olive oil
125g sweetcorn (tinned or frozen is fine)
500g smoked haddock, skinned, boned and roughly cut into chunks
300ml fish stock
200ml full-fat milk
2 tablespoons crème fraîche (optional but good if you like very creamy chowder)
1 bay leaf
Small handful of parsley, freshly chopped
Black pepper

This is a variation of the traditional chowder. I prefer to use sweetcorn rather than creamed sweetcorn. I also like to add more vegetables to make a more nutritious dish – this has sweet potato for added colour and flavour.

- Place the onion, bacon and sweet potatoes on a baking tray or in a roasting tin. Drizzle with olive oil and place in the halogen on the high rack. Cook at 210°C for 10 minutes, turning occasionally.

- Remove from the oven and place in an ovenproof casserole dish (make sure it fits in your halogen).

- Add all the remaining ingredients. Combine well. Season with black pepper – you should not need salt as the stock and fish should make it salty enough.

- Cover with a lid or double layer of foil, held securely.

- Place on the low rack and set to 190°C. Cook for 20–30 minutes before serving with crusty bread.

72

● Fish

Serves 4

One-pot Roasted Fish, Fennel and Red Onion

Preparation time:
10 minutes
Cooking time:
35 minutes

If you haven't tried fennel you really should – it is lovely and goes so well with fish.

Ingredients:
2–4 white fish fillets
Seasoning
2 lemons
1 large or 2 small bulbs fennel, sliced
2 red onions, sliced
2–3 cloves garlic, finely sliced
Olive oil
25g butter

- Prepare the fish fillets, season well and squeeze with a little lemon juice. Leave to one side until needed.

- Place the sliced fennel, onion, garlic and 1 lemon, cut into wedges, in a roasting or baking tray, making sure it fits in your halogen oven.

- Drizzle with olive oil and place in the halogen on the low rack at 220°C for 15 minutes.

- Place the fish fillets on top of the vegetables with a small knob of butter on top of each fillet. Squeeze the juice of the remaining lemon and drizzle over the dish. Season to taste.

- Cover securely with foil and bake for another 15–20 minutes until the fish is thoroughly cooked and flakes easily off the fork.

- Remove the foil and serve with new potatoes and a fresh green salad.

Fish •

Serves 4

Creamy Fish Pie

Ingredients:
1kg potatoes
500g fish fillets, or ask your fishmonger for pieces of flaky white fish
200g salmon pieces (optional)
100g prawns (optional)
250ml milk
25g butter
25g flour
1 teaspoon mustard
Seasoning to taste
A little grated cheese for topping

NB: If using salmon and prawns you can reduce the quantity of fish fillet

Another family favourite – a one-pot book wouldn't be complete without this! Why not use sweet potatoes to create a golden yet nutritious topping?

- Boil or steam the potatoes until tender. Once cooked, mash with a little butter and place to one side.

- Meanwhile place the fish, salmon, prawns and milk in a pan and bring the milk to the boil. Reduce the heat and cook gently for 10 minutes or until the fish is cooked through.

- Drain the fish and reserve the liquid for making the sauce. Shred the fish and place in a pie dish.

- To make the creamy sauce, melt the butter in a pan and add the flour. Stir in the reserved milk stock and heat gently until the sauce thickens. I normally use a whisk at this stage as it helps prevent any lumps from forming. Stir continuously. Add the mustard and season to taste.

- Pour the sauce over the fish.

- Cover the fish with mashed potato and top with a small amount of grated cheese.

- Place in the halogen on the low rack. Bake at 200°C for 20–25 minutes until golden on top.

● Fish

Serves 4

Salmon One Pot

Preparation time:
10 minutes
Cooking time:
35 minutes

I love the flavours of this one pot: asparagus, tomatoes and salmon – what a great mix.

- Place the new potatoes in a roasting dish. Drizzle with olive oil and sprinkle with paprika.

- Place in the halogen on the high rack and set the temperature to 200°C. Cook for 15–20 minutes.

- While the potatoes are cooking, add lemon zest and juice to the fillets and sprinkle with chopped tarragon. Season with black pepper.

- Remove the potatoes from the oven. Add the salmon fillets, asparagus and tomatoes. Drizzle with a little more olive oil and a dash of balsamic over the tomatoes.

- Place back in the oven, this time on the low rack, and cook at the same temperature for another 10–15 minutes or until the fish is cooked to your requirements.

- Serve immediately.

Ingredients:
700g new potatoes, halved if
    they are large
Olive oil
Paprika
4 salmon fillets
Zest and juice of ½ lemon
Small handful of tarragon,
    chopped
Black pepper
Bunch of asparagus, trimmed
200g cherry or vine tomatoes
Balsamic vinegar

Serves 4

Haddock, Egg and Gruyère Bake

Ingredients:
400g haddock fillets, roughly
  chopped
2-3 hard-boiled eggs, halved
  or quartered
200ml crème fraîche
150ml milk
125g Gruyère cheese, grated
2 teaspoons wholegrain
  mustard
Seasoning
2 tablespoons breadcrumbs
1 tablespoon oats
50g Parmesan cheese, grated

This is such a quick and easy dish and perfect for a comforting supper.

- In an ovenproof dish, making sure it fits in the halogen, place the chopped haddock and hard-boiled eggs.

- In a bowl, mix the crème fraîche, milk, grated cheese and mustard. Season to taste. Spoon this over the egg and haddock mixture.

- Mix the breadcrumbs, oats and Parmesan together, season well and sprinkle over the crème fraîche mixture.

- Place in the halogen on the low rack and bake at 180°C for 15–20 minutes, until the haddock is cooked.

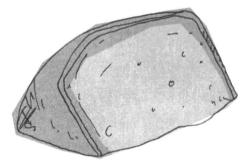

- Fish

Serves 4

Salmon and Watercress Frittata

Preparation time:
10 minutes
Cooking time:
20–25 minutes

Packed with omega 3 from the salmon, this dish can be served hot or cold.

Ingredients:
6 eggs, beaten
100ml double cream
1 small onion, finely chopped
400g tin salmon, flaked
75g watercress, chopped
Black pepper
Sea salt
Nutmeg, freshly grated

- Grease a deep dish. Place in the halogen on the high rack and set the temperature to 190°C.

- Meanwhile, combine the eggs and double cream in a large jug or bowl. Add the onion, salmon and watercress and season with black pepper, sea salt and freshly grated nutmeg.

- Open the halogen lid and carefully pour the mixture into the dish, ensuring it is evenly covered.

- Place the lid back down and cook for 20–25 minutes until golden and puffed.

- Serve with a lovely green salad.

Serves 4

Roasted Vegetable Monkfish

Ingredients:
2 red onions, cut into wedges
2 red or yellow peppers, thickly sliced
1–2 courgettes, thickly sliced
2 sweet potatoes, thickly sliced
Olive oil
2–3 sprigs rosemary
Black pepper
2–4 monkfish fillets (cut in half if large)
8 rashers thick lean bacon
12 vine tomatoes

Monkfish is no longer a cheap fish but it does have a very meaty flesh so it is more filling than other white fish.

- Place the vegetables, apart from the tomatoes, in an ovenproof dish. Drizzle with olive oil, add the rosemary sprigs and season with black pepper.

- Place in the halogen on the low rack and cook at 200°C for 15 minutes.

- Meanwhile, wrap the monkfish in bacon. (If the fillets are large you can cut them in half before wrapping.)

- Remove the vegetables from the halogen and add the tomatoes evenly amongst them. Place the monkfish on top of the vegetables. Drizzle with a little more olive oil and season to taste.

- Place a lid or double layer of foil over the dish, held securely. Return to the halogen and cook for another 20 minutes.

- Remove the lid or foil and cook again for another 5–10 minutes before serving.

Serves 4

Tuna and Sweetcorn Lasagne

Preparation time:
10 minutes
Cooking time:
45–50 minutes

An easy lasagne. Remember that you can dramatically reduce the cooking time if you use fresh pasta sheets, otherwise you may have to cover the top of the lasagne to stop it from getting too brown as it will need to cook for around 45 minutes.

- Mix the tuna, spring onions and sweetcorn together in a bowl. Season to taste.

- Add a layer of tuna mash to the bottom of a lasagne dish, cover with a layer of lasagne sheets and top with a layer of passata. Continue this process once more, ending with a layer of passata.

- Grate Parmesan or other cheese over the final layer of passata and sprinkle with black pepper.

- Place in the halogen on the low rack and cook at 210°C for 40–50 minutes until golden and the lasagne sheets are cooked. If the top starts to get too dark, cover with tin foil, making sure it is secure. (The cooking time can be greatly reduced if you use fresh lasagne sheets.)

- Serve with salad and garlic bread.

Ingredients:
400g tuna (roughly 2 tins),
    mashed
3–4 spring onions, chopped
200g sweetcorn (tinned or
    frozen)
Seasoning to taste
Lasagne sheets
500ml passata
Grated Parmesan or other
    cheese for topping

Serves 4

Tomato, Garlic and Basil Baked Cod

Ingredients:
Olive oil
1 onion, finely chopped
3 cloves garlic, finely chopped
2 tins chopped tomatoes
Small handful of basil leaves, finely chopped
Small handful of parsley, finely chopped
Seasoning to taste
4 cod fillets (or pollock, coley or any other white fish fillet)
4 slices wholemeal bread, made into breadcrumbs
50g oats
30g Parmesan cheese, grated

You can use other white fish instead of cod if you prefer.

- Heat a little oil in a sauté pan over a medium heat, add the onion and garlic and cook until the onion starts to soften.

- Add the tomatoes, herbs and seasoning and cook for another 5 minutes.

- Place the fillets in the base of your ovenproof dish and pour the tomato mixture on top.

- Mix the breadcrumbs, oats and Parmesan together and season to taste. Sprinkle this over the top of the tomato mixture.

- Place in the halogen on the low rack and cook at 190°C for 20–25 minutes until the fish is cooked.

- Serve with green salad or vegetables.

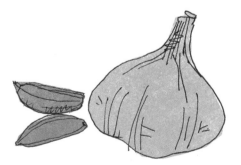

● Fish

Serves 4

Tomato and Tuna Gratin

Preparation time:
10 minutes
Cooking time:
20–25 minutes

Simple yet satisfying – and a great store cupboard standby!

- Chop the tuna into chunks and place in the bottom of an ovenproof dish.

- Heat a little olive oil in a sauté pan over a medium heat. Add the onion, garlic and red pepper and cook until they start to soften. Add the chopped tomatoes, balsamic vinegar and herbs. Season to taste. Pour this over the tuna.

- In a bowl, mix the breadcrumbs, oats and grated cheese, and season to taste. Sprinkle over the tomato mixture.

- Place in the halogen on the low rack and cook at 200°C for 15 minutes.

Ingredients:
400g tinned tuna
Olive oil
1 red onion, finely chopped
2 cloves garlic, crushed
½ red pepper, diced
1 tin chopped tomatoes
Dash of balsamic vinegar
Small handful of basil, chopped
½ teaspoon dried thyme
Seasoning to taste
75g breadcrumbs
50g oats
50g mature Cheddar, grated
Seasoning to taste

Fish •

Preparation time:
10 minutes
Cooking time:
25 minutes

Red Snapper and Tomato Bake

Ingredients:
500g red snapper fillets
Seasoning
Olive oil
2 cloves garlic, crushed
1 red onion, finely chopped
50g sundried tomatoes, chopped
3 ripe vine tomatoes
200ml red wine
Handful of fresh basil, chopped

Red snapper has a nutty flavour which works well with the tomato flavours of the sauce.

- Place the fish fillets in an ovenproof dish. Season to taste.

- Heat a little oil in a sauté pan and add the garlic and red onion. Fry until the onion starts to become translucent. (If you prefer, you can cook the onion and garlic in the halogen oven. Place on the high rack and cook on high heat until translucent. Pour this onto the fish, add the remaining ingredients, then bake as indicated below.)

- Add the tomatoes, wine and half the basil. Cook for another 2–3 minutes. Remove and pour over the fish.

- Cover the ovenproof dish with foil. Bake in the halogen on the low rack for 20 minutes at 190°C, until the fish is cooked.

- To serve, garnish with the remaining basil.

● Fish

Tomato, Prawn and Fish Stew

Preparation time:
10–15 minutes
Cooking time:
45–50 minutes

A lovely wholesome dish, perfect with fresh crusty bread.

- Heat a little oil in a sauté pan and fry the onion, garlic and pepper for 2–3 minutes.

- Select a casserole or ovenproof dish, making sure it fits well in your halogen oven. Place the onion mixture and all the remaining ingredients into your dish and combine well. Season to taste.

- Cover with a lid or piece of tin foil, secured well.

- Place in the halogen on the low rack and cook at 180°C for 40 minutes before serving.

Ingredients:
Olive oil
1 onion, finely chopped
2 cloves garlic, crushed
1 red pepper, deseeded and
  diced
1 tin chopped tomatoes, or 6
  ripe tomatoes
300ml warm fish stock
300ml white wine
520g fish fillets or pieces
12 prawns
2 bay leaves
Handful of fresh parsley,
  chopped
Seasoning to taste

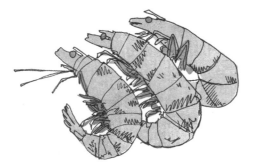

Serves 4

Cheat's Fish Biryani

Ingredients:
Olive oil
1 onion, finely chopped
2½cm knuckle ginger, finely chopped
2–3 cloves garlic, finely chopped
1 jar good quality curry sauce (use whatever strength you prefer – most jars include a strength guide)
3–4 white fish fillets, diced
Handful of coriander leaves
2 packs pilau rice (use steamed or ready cooked)

This really is a cheat's dish. If you prefer, you can make your own rice and curry paste, but I have included readymade products in this recipe as many readers like to have a quick and easy meal.

- Heat a little olive oil in a large sauté pan, add the onion, ginger and garlic and cook over a medium heat for 3–4 minutes.

- Add the curry sauce. Half fill the jar with water, rinse and add to the mixture.

- Add the fish and coriander leaves and simmer on a medium heat for 10 minutes. Remove from the heat.

- In an ovenproof dish, add a layer of the fish curry, followed by the rice. Repeat, finishing with a layer of rice.

- Sprinkle 3 tablespoons water over the top of the final layer. Finish with a double layer of foil, held securely, or pop a lid over the layer of foil as you want a secure seal.

- Place in the halogen on the low rack and cook for 15–20 minutes at 190°C.

- Serve with a selection of Indian dish accompaniments.

Serves 4

Cod and Cheese Gratin

Preparation time:
10 minutes
Cooking time:
20–25 minutes

You can use any white fish for this dish, but cod does work really well with the creamy cheese sauce.

- Mix the crème fraîche, milk, parsley, mustard and mature cheese in a bowl. Season to taste.

- Place the fish pieces in the bottom of an ovenproof dish and pour over the crème fraîche mixture.

- Mix the oats, breadcrumbs and Parmesan together. Season and sprinkle on top of the crème fraîche mixture.

- Place in the halogen on the low rack and cook at 180°C for 20–25 minutes.

Ingredients:
350ml crème fraîche
150ml milk
Small handful of fresh
  parsley, chopped
1 teaspoon wholegrain
  mustard
100g mature cheese
Seasoning to taste
3–4 skinless cod fillets,
  roughly chopped
100g oats
100g breadcrumbs
50g Parmesan, grated

Serves 4

Slow-baked Tomato and Tuna Bake

Ingredients:
Olive oil
2 cloves garlic, crushed
1 red onion, finely chopped
4-6 ripe tomatoes, quartered
Sea salt
Sugar
1 dessertspoon balsamic
  vinegar
Handful of fresh basil,
  chopped
Black pepper
300g dried pasta twirls
300g tuna, crumbled
50g mozzarella

Tuna and tomatoes are a match made in heaven.

- Place a little oil, the garlic, onion and tomatoes in an ovenproof dish. Sprinkle with sea salt, sugar and balsamic vinegar. Add half of the fresh basil. Season to taste with black pepper.

- Place in the halogen on the low rack and cook at 170°C for 20–30 minutes. Meanwhile, cook the pasta, following the instructions on the packet.

- Drain the pasta. Remove the ovenproof dish once cooked. Add the cooked pasta and crumbled tuna. Combine well. Finish with crumbled mozzarella, a drizzle of olive oil and season with black pepper.

- Bake on the low rack for 10–15 minutes at 190°C, before serving immediately.

Serves 4

Creamy Ginger and Lemon Haddock Bake

Preparation time:
10 minutes
Cooking time:
20–25 minutes

You could use smoked haddock instead for a different flavour.

- Wash and place the haddock fillets in the bottom of an ovenproof dish.

- Mix the crème fraîche, milk, lemon zest, ginger, mustard and parsley together. Season to taste. Pour over the fish fillets until evenly covered. Sprinkle the top of the bake with paprika.

- Place in the halogen on the high rack and set the temperature to 190°C. Bake for 20–25 minutes, or until the fish is cooked to your taste.

- Serve with wilted spinach.

Ingredients:
4 haddock fillets
250g crème fraîche
100ml milk
Zest of 1 lemon
2–3cm knuckle of ginger, chopped
2 teaspoons wholegrain mustard
Small handful of parsley, chopped
Seasoning
Paprika

Preparation time:
10 minutes

Cooking time
20 minutes

Serves 4

Vegetable and Halibut Pot Roast

Ingredients:
Olive oil
4 halibut fillets
2 red onions, cut into wedges
2 red peppers, cut into thick
   slices or wedges
3–4 cloves garlic, roughly
   chopped
12–16 cherry tomatoes
2 tablespoons capers
3 sprigs thyme
Balsamic vinegar
Black pepper

Halibut is rich in omega 3, protein, potassium, selenium and magnesium. Combined with the vegetables, this makes a very healthy meal for all the family.

- Drizzle a little olive oil into a deep baking tray. Place the fish, onion, red pepper, garlic and cherry tomatoes in the tray and combine until evenly distributed.

- Add the capers and thyme and drizzle again with olive oil. Finish with a sprinkle of balsamic vinegar and season with black pepper.

- Cover the tray with foil, making sure it is secure. Place in the halogen on the high rack and cook at 200°C for 20 minutes.

- Remove the foil and continue to cook for another 5 minutes.

- Serve with new potatoes.

- **Fish**

Serves 4

Cheesy Pollock Layer

Preparation time:
10–15 minutes
Cooking time:
25 minutes

A filling dish with multiple layers of flavour. Pollock has become more popular in recent years due to the over-fishing of cod and haddock. If you don't want to use pollock, however, you can opt for cod or even coley.

Ingredients:
4 pollock fillets
Juice and zest of 1 lemon
100g baby leaf spinach
3 tomatoes, sliced
Seasoning
250g crème fraîche
200ml milk
100g Parmesan cheese, grated
40g breadcrumbs
40g oats

- Squeeze the lemon juice over the fillets and leave to one side.

- In the base of an ovenproof dish, place a layer of spinach leaves and add the tomato slices on top. Season with black pepper.

- Place the fish fillets over the tomatoes. Add any remaining lemon juice and the lemon zest.

- In a bowl, mix the crème fraîche, milk and 75g grated Parmesan cheese. Season to taste before pouring over the fish fillets.

- In another bowl, mix the breadcrumbs, oats and remaining Parmesan. Mix and season well. Sprinkle this over the sauce.

- Place in the halogen on the low rack and cook at 200°C for 25 minutes until golden.

Serves 4

Salmon, Ricotta and Cheese Cannelloni

Ingredients:
50g fresh baby leaf spinach
300g salmon fillets, shredded
1 tub ricotta
Zest of 1 lemon
Small handful of fresh dill,
  finely chopped
¼ teaspoon nutmeg, grated
8 lasagne sheets
500g crème fraîche
1 small red onion, finely
  chopped
75g mature Cheddar
Seasoning
50g breadcrumbs
30g Parmesan, grated

This is such a simple dish to make but it looks impressive and tastes even better!

- Place the baby leaf spinach in a colander and run under hot water for a couple of minutes to help soften. Drain well.

- In a bowl, mix the salmon, ricotta, spinach, lemon zest, dill and nutmeg together.

- Cook the dried lasagne sheets in boiling water for 5–8 minutes, then drain. Add the salmon and ricotta mixture to one end of each sheet. Roll up firmly to form tubes and place in an ovenproof dish in a single layer, seal-end down.

- Mix the crème fraîche, onion, Cheddar and seasoning together and pour this over the cannelloni.

- Combine the breadcrumbs and Parmesan and sprinkle over the top. Place in the halogen on the low rack and cook at 190°C for 30 minutes, until the cannelloni is cooked.

- Serve with some garlic bread and green salad.

- Fish

Serves 4

Haddock, Tomato and Spinach Bake

Preparation time:
10–15 minutes
Cooking time:
25 minutes

A favourite – we all fight over the crunchy topping.

- In a sauté pan, add a little olive oil, the onion and garlic and cook for 5 minutes on a medium heat until the onion starts to soften.

- Add the chopped tomatoes. Then half fill the tin with water to rinse out the remaining tomato juice and add also. Add the oregano, season to taste and cook for another 5 minutes.

- Place the fish fillets in a buttered ovenproof dish.

- Place the spinach in a colander and run under the hot tap so it starts to wilt slightly. Drain well. Place over the fillets. Season with black pepper. Pour the tomato mixture over the spinach.

- In your food processor, whizz the bread to form breadcrumbs. Add the oats, seeds and Cheddar cheese. Season with black pepper.

- Sprinkle this over the top of the tomato mixture. Finish with the grated Parmesan.

- Place the dish in the halogen on the low rack and cook at 180°C for 15 minutes. Serve immediately.

Ingredients:
Olive oil
1 red onion, finely chopped
2–3 cloves garlic, crushed
1 tin chopped tomatoes
½ teaspoon dried oregano, or very small handful of fresh, finely chopped
Seasoning
3–4 haddock fillets
60g baby leaf spinach
Black pepper
4 slices bread, ideally slightly stale
60g oats
40g pumpkin seeds
30g sunflower seeds
60g mature Cheddar
30g Parmesan, grated

Ingredients:
200g butter
1 tablespoon olive oil
3–4 cloves garlic, crushed
Zest and juice of 1 lemon
Small handful of flat leaf
  parsley, freshly chopped
Black pepper
750g prawns
Extra flat leaf parsley to
  garnish

Serves 4

Baked Garlic Butter Prawns

Such a simple dish, but if you like prawns you will become addicted to this recipe!

- Place the butter and olive oil in an ovenproof dish and add the garlic.

- Place in the halogen on the low rack and set the temperature to 250°C. Once the butter starts to melt remove immediately – do not walk away from this as it takes only a minute.

- Stir in the lemon zest, juice and parsley. Season to taste with black pepper.

- Place the prawns into the dish with the butter. Toss gently to ensure they are all coated.

- Cover with a lid or double layer of tinfoil. Place back in the halogen and cook at 190°C for 10 minutes or until the prawns are cooked to your taste (cooking time depends on the size and type of prawns used).

- Serve with a garnish of parsley.

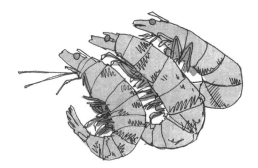

- Fish

Serves 4

Italian-style Baked Coley

You can use any white fish fillets with this dish — the choice is yours.

- Heat a little olive oil in a sauté pan. Add the onion and garlic and cook over a medium heat until the onion starts to soften.

- Add the chopped tomatoes. Then half fill the tin to rinse out the remaining tomato juice and add to the pan also. Add the white wine, olives, capers and herbs and simmer over a medium heat for 10 minutes. Season to taste.

- Place the fish in the bottom of a buttered ovenproof dish.

- Pour on the tomato mixture. Cover with a lid or double layer of foil, securely held.

- Place in the halogen on the low rack and cook at 200°C for 15–20 minutes until the fish is cooked through.

- Serve with a salad and new potatoes.

Preparation time:
10 minutes
Cooking time:
35 minutes

Ingredients:
Olive oil
1 large red onion, finely chopped
3 cloves garlic, crushed
1 tin chopped tomatoes
100ml white wine
50g olives
Small handful of capers (optional)
Small handful of basil leaves, finely chopped
Small handful of parsley leaves, finely chopped
Seasoning to taste
3-4 fish fillets

Serves 4

Tomato and Monkfish Bake

Ingredients:
250g vine tomatoes
2 red onions, cut into wedges
2–3 cloves garlic, roughly
chopped
Olive oil
Balsamic vinegar
4 tablespoons butter, melted
1–2 tablespoons wholegrain
mustard
Black pepper
4 monkfish fillets
4–5 tablespoons wholemeal
breadcrumbs
2 tablespoons grated
Parmesan

Monkfish is a great source of protein and does contain some omega 3. Serve this dish with green vegetables for a delicious meal.

- Place the tomatoes, onion and garlic in an ovenproof dish. Drizzle with olive oil and a dash of balsamic vinegar.

- Melt the butter and stir in the mustard and black pepper. Brush this over the monkfish, ensuring it is well coated.

- Sprinkle the breadcrumbs and parmesan over the fillets to form a crispy coating.

- Place the fillets over the tomatoes.

- Place in the halogen on the low rack, set to 190°C and cook for 15–20 minutes, until the fish is cooked and flakes easily.

- Serve with a green salad.

Serves 4

Vegetable and Herb Baked Cod

Preparation time:
10–15 minutes
Cooking time:
30 minutes

Imagine a ratatouille with extra herbs and baked cod on top. This is the dish – delicious.

- Place the vegetables and tomatoes in an ovenproof dish.

- Place the fish in amongst the vegetables.

- Mix the herbs with the olive oil and drizzle over the vegetables and fish. Toss well and add more olive oil if necessary.

- Cover with a lid or double layer of foil.

- Place in the halogen on the low rack and cook at 190°C for 20–30 minutes.

Ingredients:
2 red onions, cut into thick
    slices or wedges
2–3 cloves garlic, roughly
    chopped
1 pepper, thickly sliced
2 courgettes, thickly sliced
1 sweet potato, thickly sliced
½ aubergine, thickly sliced
150g vine tomatoes, left
    whole
4 fillets cod
Small handful of basil leaves,
    oregano and flat leaf
    parsley, finely chopped
2–3 tablespoons olive oil

Serves 4

Spinach and Salmon Mornay

Ingredients:
2 tablespoons butter
2 tablespoons plain flour
350ml milk
110g Gruyère cheese, grated
1 tablespoon wholegrain
   mustard
Black pepper
60g baby leaf spinach
225g salmon, flaked
50g breadcrumbs
25g Parmesan, grated

A delicious comforting supper, with the added benefit of omega 3 from the salmon. If you are watching your weight you may want to opt for low-fat cheese.

- In a saucepan over a medium heat, melt the butter. Using a wooden spoon stir in the flour and keep stirring until it starts to form a paste. Gradually add the milk and continue to stir. If lumps start to form, switch to a balloon whisk and beat well.

- When the sauce starts to thicken, you can add the grated cheese, wholegrain mustard and black pepper to taste. Leave to one side and start to prepare the rest of the dish.

- Place the spinach in a colander and wash under hot water so it starts to wilt. Then place the spinach in the bottom of a greased ovenproof dish (or individual ramekin dishes).

- Place the flaked fish into the dish and cover with the cheese sauce.

- Finish with a sprinkle of breadcrumbs and Parmesan. Season again with black pepper.

- Place in the halogen on the high rack and set the temperature to 200°C. Cook for 15 minutes until golden and bubbling.

- Serve immediately.

- **Fish**

Creamy Fish Crumble

Preparation time:
10–15 minutes

Cooking time
40–50 minutes

I really love savoury crumbles. Be adventurous and add some crunchy mixed seeds and nuts for a wholesome topping.

- Place the fish and milk in a pan and bring the milk to the boil. Reduce the heat and cook gently for 10 minutes or until the fish is cooked through.

- Drain the fish and reserve the liquid for making the sauce. Shred the fish and place in an ovenproof dish.

- To make a creamy sauce: melt 25g butter in a pan over a medium heat and add the flour. Stir in the reserved milk stock and heat gently until the sauce thickens. I normally use a whisk at this stage as it helps prevent any lumps from forming. Stir continuously. Add the mustard and season to taste. Pour the sauce over the fish.

- In a bowl, add the wholemeal flour and the butter. Rub until you form a texture similar to breadcrumbs. Add the oats, breadcrumbs, seeds and Parmesan. Season well and combine.

- Cover the fish with the crumble mix until evenly coated.

- Set the halogen to 200°C and place the crumble on the high rack. Cook for 25–30 minutes until golden and bubbling.

- Serve immediately with a green salad.

Ingredients:
500g fish fillets, or ask your
    fishmonger for pieces of
    flaky white fish
200g salmon pieces (optional)
100g prawns (optional)
250ml milk
25g butter
25g flour
1 teaspoon mustard
Seasoning to taste

Crumble Ingredients
100g wholemeal flour
50g butter
75g oats
75g wholemeal breadcrumbs
50g mixed seeds (optional)
50g Parmesan cheese, grated

Serves 4

Creamy Haddock Pie with Crisp Rosti Topping

Ingredients:
4 eggs
400ml milk
Bay leaf
Black pepper
450g haddock
1 dessertspoon butter
1 dessertspoon flour
2 teaspoons wholegrain
    mustard
Small handful of parsley,
    freshly chopped
600g potatoes
50g butter
50g Parmesan
50g breadcrumbs

If you like fish pie you'll love this version with a crunchy rosti topping.

- Hard-boil the eggs: cook them for 6–7 minutes, then place them in cold water and leave to one side.

- Meanwhile, in another saucepan, add the milk, bay leaf, black pepper to taste and haddock pieces. Bring to the boil, then reduce the heat and simmer for 10 minutes, or until the fish is cooked (it should flake easily).

- Drain the fish and retain the milk for later. Remove the bay leaf and discard. You can reuse the same saucepan so no need to wash up!

- In the saucepan over a medium heat, melt 1 dessertspoon butter and add the flour to form a paste, gradually adding the warm milk until you form a smooth sauce. Continue to stir well until it starts to thicken. If lumps start to form, switch to a balloon whisk and beat well.

- Add the mustard and season to taste. Stir in the chopped parsley.

- Place the fish in the bottom of an ovenproof dish. Chop the boiled eggs and add to the dish. Pour on the sauce and combine well.

- Grate the potatoes with a coarse grater. Melt 50g butter and combine with the potatoes. Season to taste.

- Fish

- Spoon this over the fish. Finish with a sprinkle of Parmesan and a sprinkle of breadcrumbs.

- When you are ready to cook, place in the halogen on the high rack. Set to 200°C and cook for 25 minutes until golden.

CHAPTER 5

Vegetarian

Vegetarian dishes aren't just for vegetarians! Try the recipes in this chapter and I am sure you will love them. It is good to have at least two vegetarian meals a week – alternate with fresh oily fish and cut down your red meat consumption. Some of these dishes are suitable for vegans – see the notes included in the recipes for advice.

Serves 4

Roasted Tomato, Pepper and Sweet Potato Soup

Using the halogen is the best way to roast vegetables. This soup is delicious. You could double up the quantity of vegetables and set the extra portion aside to use as a pizza topping or with some pasta.

- Place the vegetables in the roasting tray. Drizzle with olive oil and spread the thyme in amongst the vegetables.

- Place in the halogen on the high rack and cook at 190°C for 20–25 minutes.

- Remove and scrape everything into a saucepan, discarding the thyme if burnt and woody.

- Add the stock and season to taste. Liquidise gently using an electric stick blender.

- Bring to the boil and simmer gently for 5 minutes before serving.

Ingredients:
2 red onions, cut into thick wedges
2 red peppers, cut into thick wedges
1 sweet potato, thickly sliced
3 cloves garlic, left whole
250–300g vine tomatoes, left whole
Olive oil
3–4 sprigs thyme
400ml vegetable stock
Seasoning to taste

Vegetarian •

Serves 4

Veggie Hot Pot

Ingredients:
1 red onion, finely chopped
2 red peppers, finely sliced
3 cloves garlic, roughly
  chopped
1 punnet cherry tomatoes
1 tin haricot beans (or
  chickpeas or borlotti)
150ml red wine (or vegetable
  stock)
1 teaspoon paprika
1–2 teaspoons oregano,
  freshly chopped
100g low-fat feta cheese,
  crumbled
3–4 large potatoes, finely
  sliced
Black pepper
30g Parmesan cheese, grated

A variation of the traditional hotpot, this is a really simple dish and absolutely delicious. I love the crusty, golden top contrasting with the tomato and herb base.

- Place the onion, peppers, garlic, tomatoes and beans in a casserole dish (make sure the dish fits in your halogen).

- Add the wine, paprika and oregano and combine well.

- Sprinkle the crumbled feta over the top of the vegetables.

- Layer with the sliced potatoes and season well with black pepper. Sprinkle with Parmesan cheese.

- Place in the halogen on the low rack and set to 180°C. Cook for 30–40 minutes or until the potatoes are cooked and golden. If the top starts to get too dark, cover with a lid or double layer of foil, held securely.

● **Vegetarian**

Serves 4

Quorn and Spinach Curry

Preparation time:
10 minutes
Cooking time:
30 minutes

Quorn is a fantastic, low-fat food, mainly used by vegetarians (though not suitable for vegans), but it is a great food for everyone and a cheaper, healthier alternative to meat.

- Spray an ovenproof dish with a little olive oil. Add the onion and pepper and spray with a little more oil.

- Place in the halogen on the high rack, set to 200°C and cook for about 5 minutes.

- Add the garlic, ginger and chilli and cook for another 5 minutes. Remove from the oven and add the Quorn, curry powder, tomatoes, water/stock and mushrooms.

- Cover with a lid or double layer of foil, securely held. Place back in the halogen and cook for 10–15 minutes.

- Remove from the oven, add the spinach and chopped coriander, and season to taste. Then cook for another 5 minutes before serving.

- Serve with rice.

Ingredients:
Olive oil spray
1 large red onion, diced
1 pepper, diced
2 cloves garlic, crushed
1 teaspoon grated ginger
1 chilli, finely chopped
400g Quorn chunks
2 tablespoons medium curry powder
1 × 400g tin chopped tomatoes
300ml water or vegetable stock
100g mushrooms, quartered or baby mushrooms
400g baby spinach leaves
Small handful of coriander leaves, chopped
Seasoning

Preparation time:
15 minutes
Cooking time
45–50 minutes

Serves 4–6

Eco-Warrior Pie

Ingredients:
3 large potatoes
2 sweet potatoes
1–2 carrots, cut into mini
sticks
1–2 leeks, thinly sliced
8–10 small broccoli florets
(optional)
25g butter
25g plain flour or cornflour
250ml milk
75–100g mature Cheddar,
grated
1–2 tablespoons Nutritional
Yeast Flakes (optional)
1 teaspoon mustard
Black pepper
1–2 handfuls of spinach
leaves

This is a delicious vegetarian version of a shepherd's pie using wonderful fresh vegetables covered in a cheese sauce and topped with sweet potato mash.

- I use a large steamer to prepare the vegetables as I can steam them all using one hob. First, peel and cut the potatoes into chunks or slices (this cuts down on cooking time) and steam until soft. Then add the carrots, cut into small sticks. In the last 5–8 minutes of steaming, add the leeks and broccoli.

- To make the cheese sauce, melt the butter in a saucepan over a medium heat. Add the flour and stir to form a paste. Gradually add the milk and stir well. I find it best to switch to a balloon whisk at this point as it removes any unwanted lumps. Keep stirring until the sauce thickens.

- Add the grated cheese, mustard and season to taste. If you are using Nutritional Yeast Flakes, add these before the grated cheese as they will reduce the amount of cheese you will need – taste as you go!

- Mash the potatoes with a little milk or butter and season with black pepper.

- Place the tomato slices in the base of an ovenproof dish or 4–6 individual dishes. Cover with a thin layer of uncooked spinach leaves.

- Cover with the leeks, broccoli and carrots and coat with your cheese sauce. Finally add your mash on top.

- Vegetarian

- Place in the halogen on the low rack and cook at 200°C for 15 minutes until golden.

> **Top Tip**: If you don't want to make a cheese sauce, you could mix crème fraîche with some mature Cheddar. Personally I like the flavour of the cheese sauce.

Ingredients:
1 punnet cherry tomatoes,
  halved
2-3 cloves garlic, crushed
1 red onion, sliced
Handful of basil leaves,
  crushed
1 teaspoon salt
1 teaspoon sugar
Drizzle of olive oil
1 ball mozzarella or 80g goat's
  cheese, crumbled (omit if
  vegan and substitute with
  vegan cheese if desired)

Basic dough recipe
500g strong bread flour
325ml warm water
1 sachet dried yeast
1 teaspoon brown sugar
2 tablespoons olive oil

Serves 4–6. Suitable for vegans

Upside-down Pizza Bake

This is a really nice dish and makes a change from the normal pizza. It follows the same principle as an upside-down cake. I love the flavour of the slow-cooked tomatoes – ideal for using up some soft tomatoes. This recipe uses cherry tomatoes, but feel free to use a variety of your choice.

- Place the tomatoes, garlic, onion, basil, salt, sugar and olive oil in a deep-sided baking tray (ideally round so you can turn it out on a serving plate when complete, but make sure it fits in your halogen cooker!).

- Place in the halogen on the high rack and cook at 130–140°C for 30–40 minutes.

- Meanwhile, prepare the dough by sifting the flour into a bowl.

- Mix the water, yeast, sugar and oil together. Make sure the sugar is dissolved. Make a well in the middle of the flour and pour in.

- Mix thoroughly before transferring the dough onto a floured board. Knead well until the dough springs back when pulled.

- Place the dough in a floured bowl and cover with cling film or a warm, damp cloth until it has doubled in size. This takes about 1 hour.

- Knead again. Roll out to form the same size as your baking tray (you will later place the dough inside the tray to form a top). You may have more dough than needed, it depends on how thick you

- Vegetarian

want the crust of the bake. If you have some left over, you can roll it out to make a pizza base, cover in greased foil or parchment and freeze for another day.

- Remove the baked tomatoes from the halogen oven and turn up to 200°C. You can top the tomatoes with the dough, or for cheese lovers you may like to add some sliced mozzarella or even crumbled goat's cheese onto the tomatoes before adding the dough.

- Return to the halogen and bake for 15–20 minutes until the top is golden.

- To serve, place a plate, slightly larger than the top of the baking tray, over the dough, face down, ready to flip up, displaying the tomato base on top of the pizza dough.

- Serve with green salad.

Serves 4

Vegetable and Tomato Pot Roast

Ingredients:

1-2 onions, cut into thick
   wedges
350g new potatoes, halved if
   they are large
Olive oil
1-2 red peppers, cut into
   wedges
2 carrots, cut into sticks
2 sweet potatoes, cut into
   thick wedges or slices
4 cloves garlic, left whole
Olive oil
Black pepper
Sea salt
3-4 sprigs rosemary or thyme
2 courgettes, cut into wedges
½ punnet vine or cherry
   tomatoes
1 tin chopped tomatoes or 1
   jar pasta sauce

This is a dish where anything goes really – great for using up any odd vegetables in your fridge. You can use a tin of tomatoes or a tin of good quality pasta sauce.

- Place the onions and new potatoes in a roasting dish, drizzle with olive oil and place in the halogen on the high rack. Set the temperature to 210°C and cook for 15 minutes.

- Add all remaining ingredients apart from the chopped tomatoes or pasta sauce. Drizzle with more oil and season with black pepper and sea salt. Place back in the oven for another 15–20 minutes, until the potatoes are golden.

- When the vegetables are cooked and the potatoes are golden, remove from the oven and stir in the chopped tomatoes or pasta sauce.

- Place back in the oven for another 10 minutes before serving. Note: If you are a cheese lover you could crumble some feta or goat's cheese on top before serving.

● Vegetarian

Serves 4–6

Vegetable Mornay Bake

Preparation time:
10 minutes
Cooking time:
40–45 minutes

A family favourite, suitable as a main meal or even a side dish.

- Chop the carrots into sticks, slice the leeks and cut the broccoli and cauliflower into manageable florets. Place in a steamer and cook until the cauliflower is tender but not soft.

- Meanwhile, make the sauce. Melt the butter gently in a saucepan over a medium heat (not high!). Add the flour or cornflour and stir well with a wooden spoon. Add the milk a little at a time, continuing to stir to avoid lumps.

- Switch now to a balloon whisk. Continue to stir over a medium heat until the sauce begins to thicken. The balloon whisk will also help to eradicate any lumps that may have formed. The sauce should be the thickness of custard; add more milk as necessary.

- If you are using nutritional yeast flakes, add these before the grated cheese as they will reduce the amount of cheese you will need – taste as you go! Then add the cheese and mustard and stir well. Season with black pepper.

- When the vegetables are ready, transfer them to an ovenproof dish. Pour over the sauce ensuring all the vegetables are covered.

- Mix the oats, breadcrumbs and Parmesan together thoroughly. Scatter over the cheese sauce.

- Place the mornay in the halogen on the low rack. Cook at 210°C for 15–20 minutes until the top is golden and crispy.

Ingredients:
2 carrots
2 leeks
1 small broccoli
1 small cauliflower
25g butter
1 tablespoon plain flour or cornflour
500–750ml milk
2 tablespoons nutritional yeast flakes (optional)
100g mature cheese, grated (75g for the sauce, 25g for the topping)
½ teaspoon mustard
Black pepper
2 tablespoons oats
2–3 tablespoons home-prepared wholemeal breadcrumbs
25g Parmesan cheese

Serves 2

Roasted Vegetable and Mozzarella Tortilla Layer

Ingredients:
1 red onion, thickly sliced
1-2 cloves garlic, roughly
    chopped (optional)
1-2 red peppers, thickly sliced
1-2 courgettes, thickly sliced
8-12 cherry tomatoes
Olive oil
1 sprig thyme
Seasoning
50g sweetcorn
1 pack tortilla wraps
1 ball mozzarella, diced or
    crumbled
A little milk or beaten egg
Small handful of grated
    cheese

I love roasted vegetables as they are so easy in the halogen. I normally double up the batch and keep some in the fridge – a perfect quick and easy snack for hungry teens.

- In an ovenproof dish, place the onion, garlic, pepper, courgette and tomatoes.

- Drizzle with olive oil and add the sprig of thyme. Season to taste.

- Place in the halogen on the high rack and set to 200°C. Cook for 15–20 minutes.

- Remove from the oven and stir in the sweetcorn.

- In a small round ovenproof dish, place a tortilla wrap, add a few spoonfuls of the roasted veg, followed by a few chunks of mozzarella. Add another tortilla wrap. Continue this to fill the dish, finishing with a tortilla wrap.

- Brush the top with milk or beaten egg. Sprinkle with grated cheese.

- Place on the low rack and cook at 200°C for 10–15 minutes.

- Slice and serve with a salad.

- Vegetarian

Serves 4–6

Mushroom and Cottage Cheese Lasagne

Preparation time:
10 minutes
Cooking time:
50 minutes

If you like mushrooms you will love this lasagne. To help speed up the cooking time, opt for fresh pasta sheets or you could boil the lasagne sheets before placing in the dish.

Ingredients:
10ml olive oil
1 onion, finely chopped
1–2 cloves garlic
250g mushrooms, quartered
1 teaspoon dried thyme (or fresh thyme if you have it)
1 tub cottage cheese
Lasagne sheets
Grated Parmesan or other cheese for topping
Black pepper to taste

- Heat the olive oil in a large sauté pan and fry the onion and garlic until the onion becomes translucent. Add the mushrooms and cook for another 5 minutes.

- Remove from the heat and stir in the thyme and cottage cheese. Leave to one side.

- Place a layer of mushroom mix in a lasagne dish, followed by a layer of lasagne sheets, and alternate the two, finishing with a layer of lasagne. If you boil the lasagne sheets for 5–8 minutes before adding to the dish, you can reduce the cooking time to 25–30 minutes.

- Grate some Parmesan or other cheese onto the lasagne and season.

- Place in the halogen oven on the low rack and cook at 200°C for 40–50 minutes. If the top starts to get too dark, cover with tin foil, making sure it is secure.

- Serve with potato wedges and salad – delicious!

Serves 4

Ratatouille and Feta Gratin

Ingredients:
1 aubergine, diced
1 red onion, sliced
2 cloves garlic, crushed
1 red pepper, roughly diced
1 courgette, diced
8 ripe tomatoes, quartered (or tinned if you prefer)
Olive oil
Sprinkle of sugar
2–3 teaspoons balsamic vinegar
100ml red wine
Sprigs of thyme
Small handful of bay leaves
Seasoning
75g wholemeal breadcrumbs
50g oats
50g Parmesan cheese, grated
120g feta cheese, crumbled

I love the crispy bake topping of this dish.

- In an ovenproof dish, add the prepared vegetables. Drizzle with olive oil, sugar, balsamic vinegar, wine, herbs and season. Combine to ensure all the vegetables are covered in a little oil.

- Bake in the halogen on the low rack at 210°C for 20–30 minutes until the vegetables are soft.

- Meanwhile, mix together the breadcrumbs, oats and Parmesan. Season to taste.

- Remove the vegetables from the oven and stir in the feta cheese. Finish with the breadcrumb mix.

- Return to the low rack and cook for another 15 minutes until golden.

● **Vegetarian**

Serves 4–6

Sundried Tomato and Goat's Cheese Fritatta

Preparation time:
10 minutes
Cooking time:
20–25 minutes

This is an ideal dish for using up any leftover cooked potatoes.

- In a large bowl, add the eggs and beat well. Add the remaining ingredients and combine.

- Pour into a well-greased ovenproof dish. Place in the halogen on the low rack and cook at 200°C for 20–25 minutes until it is firm.

- Serve hot or cold with salad.

Ingredients:
5 eggs, beaten
4–5 spring onions, finely
  chopped
110g goat's cheese, crumbled
4–6 sundried tomatoes,
  chopped
1 teaspoon mixed herbs
Seasoning to taste

Serves 4

Italian Crunch Hotpot

Ingredients:
Olive oil
1 red onion, chopped
3 cloves garlic, crushed
1 red pepper, thickly diced
2 courgettes, thickly sliced
½ aubergine, diced
1 tin chopped tomatoes
2 teaspoons tomato purée
1 tin haricot beans or
　　chickpeas
½ teaspoons dried oregano
½ teaspoons dried marjoram
200ml red wine
Seasoning to taste
½ stick of French bread or
　　ciabatta, thinly sliced
30g Parmesan cheese (or if
　　you like thick golden cheesy
　　crusts, use 50g mature
　　Cheddar), grated

I love this dish – the topping is to die for and we all argue over the crispiest pieces.

- In a sauté pan, add a drizzle of olive oil followed by the onion, garlic and pepper. Cook over a medium heat for 5 minutes until the onion starts to soften before adding all the remaining ingredients apart from the bread and cheese.

- Simmer for 15 minutes.

- Remove from the heat and pour the mixture into an ovenproof dish.

- Arrange the sliced bread over the top of the mixture. Finish with the grated cheese and black pepper.

- Place in the halogen oven on the low rack. Set to 190°C and cook for 10 minutes until golden and bubbling.

● Vegetarian

Serves 4–6

Spinach and Ricotta Cannelloni

Preparation time:
10 minutes
Cooking time:
50 minutes

This is such a simple dish to make but looks impressive and tastes even better!

- Place the spinach in a colander and run under hot water for a couple of minutes to help soften. If you are using frozen spinach, allow it to defrost before moving on to the next step.

- In a bowl, mix the ricotta, baby leaf spinach and nutmeg together. Using a teaspoon, fill the cannelloni tubes with the ricotta mixture. (If you want to speed up the cooking time you can use fresh cannelloni tubes or dried lasagne sheets. Cook the dried lasagne sheets in boiling water for 5–8 minutes, before draining. Add the spinach and ricotta to one end of each sheet. Roll up firmly to form tubes, placing the seal on the bottom of the ovenproof dish.) Place the stuffed tubes in an ovenproof dish in a single layer.

- Fry the onion and garlic in a little olive oil to help soften. Add the tomatoes, wine, basil and seasoning and cook for a couple of minutes before pouring this over the cannelloni. Sprinkle with Parmesan.

- Place in the halogen on the low rack. Cook at 190°C for 35–40 minutes, until the cannelloni is cooked (this takes 20–25 minutes if you are using fresh pasta or lasagne sheets as above).

- Serve with garlic bread and green salad.

Ingredients:
150g fresh baby leaf spinach (or use 300g frozen)
1 tub ricotta
¼ teaspoon nutmeg, grated
Cannelloni tubes or lasagne sheets
Olive oil
1 small red onion
2 cloves garlic, crushed
1 tin chopped tomatoes
75ml red wine
Handful of basil leaves, freshly chopped
Seasoning
Parmesan, grated

Serves 4

Potato, Cheese and Onion Layer

Ingredients:
1kg potatoes, very thinly
    sliced
2 onions, thinly sliced
3 cloves garlic, crushed
150g mature Cheddar, grated
Paprika
Black pepper
100g low-fat crème fraîche
2 eggs
100ml milk
Nutmeg

This can be served hot or cold.

- Boil the potato slices for 5 minutes to help speed up the cooking process. Drain and leave until needed.

- Grease a deep ovenproof dish.

- Place a thin layer of potato, followed by a layer of onion, a sprinkle of garlic and a layer of cheese. Follow this with a sprinkle of paprika and season with black pepper (you don't need to add salt as the cheese is salty enough). Continue layering until the dish is three-quarters full.

- In a bowl or jug, mix the crème fraîche with the eggs and milk. Season with black pepper and nutmeg. Pour this over the potato layers.

- Place the dish in the halogen on the low rack. Set to 210°C and cook for 30–40 minutes or until the potatoes are cooked.

- Serve with a lovely salad.

- Vegetarian

Vegetable Crumble

Preparation time:
15 minutes
Cooking time:
40 minutes

This is a very filling one-pot dish packed with goodness. Serve on its own or with a salad for a perfect meal.

- Place the potatoes and carrot in a steamer and steam for 10 minutes to help soften.

- Meanwhile, place a little olive oil in a pan and sauté the onion and garlic until they start to soften. Add the pepper, celery, chopped tomatoes, vegetable stock, spinach and herbs and cook for 10 minutes.

- Add the potatoes and carrot to the tomato mixture and season to taste. Pour this into an ovenproof dish, making sure it fits well in your halogen oven.

- In a bowl, add the flour and rub in the butter to form a texture similar to breadcrumbs. Add the grated cheese and season.

- Sprinkle this over the vegetable base. Place the crumble on the low rack and cook at 180°C for 20 minutes until golden and bubbling.

- Serve immediately.

Ingredients:
1 sweet potato, diced
1 potato, diced
2 carrots, diced
Olive oil
1 onion, finely chopped
2–3 cloves garlic, finely chopped
1 red pepper, diced
1 stick celery, diced
1 tin chopped tomatoes
200ml vegetable stock
1–2 handfuls of fresh baby leaf spinach
Small handful of mixed fresh herbs
Seasoning to taste
75g butter (or vegan spread)
175g plain flour
50g mature Cheddar, grated (if vegan, omit the cheese or substitute with a sprinkle of nutritional yeast flakes or vegan cheese)

Serves 4

Roasted Butternut, Spinach and Goat's Cheese Layer

Ingredients:
2 teaspoons coriander seeds
1 teaspoon cumin seeds
1 butternut squash, peeled, deseeded and sliced
Olive oil
1–2 chillies, finely chopped (depending on desired strength)
2 red onions, sliced
3–4 cloves garlic, chopped
50–75g baby leaf spinach
1 tub ricotta
Seasoning to taste
1–2 ripe tomatoes, sliced
25g pine nuts
110g goat's cheese, crumbled

This may take a little time to prepare, but other than chopping, the halogen does the hard work for you. It tastes amazing and will impress even the most ardent meat eaters!

- Using a pestle and mortar, roughly grind the coriander and cumin seeds.

- Place the squash slices on a baking tray and drizzle with olive oil. Sprinkle with the coriander seeds, cumin and chilli.

- Place in the halogen on the low rack, set to 210°C and roast for 15 minutes. Remove and add the onion and garlic. Place back in the halogen and cook for another 15 minutes.

- Meanwhile, you can prepare the rest of the layers. Rinse the spinach leaves under a hot tap to soften. Place in a bowl and mix in the ricotta. Season to taste and leave to one side.

- Remove the squash and onions from the oven. Drain off any excess oil and combine the squash, onion and garlic. Place half in the bottom of an ovenproof dish.

- Add a layer of the spinach and ricotta mix. Follow this with a layer of sliced tomatoes. Then add the rest of the squash, ricotta mixture, pine nuts and finish with the crumbled goat's cheese.

- Place on the low rack and bake for 20 minutes.

- Serve with a selection of delicious salads.

- Vegetarian

Serves 4

Roasted Ratatouille Crumble

Preparation time:
10–15 minutes
Cooking time:
45 minutes

I love this dish. Make it in advance or double up the recipe, using half as a crumble and freezing the other half to serve as a normal ratatouille. For cheese addicts, you could add some crumbled feta or goat's cheese before adding the crumble topping. Yummy!

- In an ovenproof dish, combine all the vegetables. Pour over a drizzle of olive oil, a dash of balsamic and a sprinkle of sea salt and sugar. Add the herb sprigs and toss again to ensure it is all evenly coated.

- Place in the halogen on the high rack and cook at 200°C for 30 minutes.

- Meanwhile, combine the breadcrumbs, oats, pumpkin seeds and Parmesan. Season to taste.

- Remove the vegetables, add the passata and combine well. Season with black pepper. (Add some crumbled feta or goat's cheese now, if you are a cheese addict!)

- Cover with the crumble mix and place back in the oven for another 15 minutes.

- Serve immediately.

Ingredients:
2 red peppers, cut into thick
  wedges
2 red onions, cut into wedges
4–5 cloves garlic, halved
8–10 tomatoes, scored but
  left whole
1 small aubergine, cut into
  thick wedges
2 courgettes, cut into
  lengthways wedges
Olive oil
Balsamic vinegar
Sea salt
Sugar
Sprigs of fresh thyme and
  rosemary
2 tablespoons breadcrumbs
2 tablespoons oats
1 tablespoon pumpkin seeds
2 tablespoons Parmesan
  cheese, finely grated
Black pepper
1 jar passata
Feta or goat's cheese,
  crumbled (optional)

Preparation time:
10 minutes

Cooking time:
30–40 minutes

Blue Cheese and Broccoli Frittata

Ingredients:
1 head broccoli, cut into
    florets
8 eggs, beaten
100ml double cream
1 small onion, finely chopped
175g blue cheese, crumbled
Chives, freshly chopped
Black pepper
Sea salt

A lovely, quick and easy supper dish.

- Place the broccoli florets in boiling water and cook for 5–8 minutes.

- Grease a deep ovenproof dish. Place it in the halogen on the medium rack and set the temperature to 190°C.

- Meanwhile, combine the eggs and double cream in a large jug or bowl. Add the onion, broccoli, blue cheese and chives and season with black pepper and sea salt.

- Open the halogen lid carefully and pour the mixture into the dish, ensuring it is evenly distributed.

- Place the lid back down and cook for 20–25 minutes until golden and puffed.

- Serve with a lovely green salad.

- Vegetarian

Serves 4

Healthy Roasted Vegetable Lasagne

This is a really lovely dish, using low-fat quark instead of a full-fat cheese sauce. The roasted vegetables add great flavour. For extra speed, use fresh lasagne sheets as this will cut the cooking time by half.

- Place the vegetables, tomatoes and olives in an ovenproof dish. Drizzle with olive oil and a little balsamic vinegar. Add the thyme sprigs and season to taste.

- Place in the halogen on the low rack and cook at 200°C for 20 minutes, shaking or turning halfway through cooking.

- Meanwhile, mix the quark, milk, crème fraîche and Parmesan cheese together. Season to taste.

- When the vegetables are cooked, you are ready to put the lasagne together. Place some of the vegetable mixture in the base of your dish. Add a layer of lasagne sheets, followed by a few spoonfuls of the quark mixture. Repeat, finishing with the quark mixture. If you wish, sprinkle mature Cheddar over the top.

- Cover with a lid or foil, securely held, to stop the top of the lasagne from burning. Place on the low rack at 190°C for 45–50 minutes, and remove the lid or foil for the last 10 minutes of the cooking time. If you are using fresh lasagne sheets you will only need to cook for 20–25 minutes, and there's no need to cover the dish.

- Serve with a green salad and garlic bread.

Preparation time:
10–15 minutes

Cooking time:
1 hour, 20 minutes

Ingredients:
2 red onions, thickly sliced or cut into wedges
2–3 cloves garlic, roughly chopped
1 red pepper, thickly sliced
1 yellow pepper, thickly sliced
2 courgettes, thickly sliced
½ aubergine, thickly sliced
1 sweet potato, thickly sliced
150g tomatoes, left whole
40g olives, halved and destoned (optional)
Olive oil
Balsamic vinegar
2–3 sprigs thyme
Black pepper
300g quark
200ml milk
3 tablespoons low-fat crème fraîche
60g Parmesan cheese, grated
Lasagne sheets (use fresh to reduce the cooking time)
Mature Cheddar (optional), grated

Serves 4

Simple Mixed Bean and Vegetable Crumble

Ingredients:
Olive oil
1 large red onion, finely sliced
3 cloves garlic, crushed
1 red pepper, diced
2 sticks of celery, diced
1 carrot, diced
1 small sweet potato, diced
400g tin mixed beans, drained
1 tin chopped tomatoes
2 teaspoons sundried tomato
 purée
200ml red wine or vegetable
 stock
1 tablespoon thyme, freshly
 chopped
1 tablespoon marjoram,
 freshly chopped
Seasoning to taste

Crumble ingredients
100g wholemeal flour
50g butter
75g oats
75g wholemeal breadcrumbs
50g mixed seeds
50g Parmesan cheese, grated

Beans offer a great source of protein, keeping you feeling fuller for longer. They are also high in fibre, nutrients and aid digestion.

- In a saucepan (or hobproof and ovenproof casserole dish if you have one), add a drizzle of oil and place on the hob over a medium heat. Add the onion, garlic and pepper and cook until they start to soften.

- Add the celery, carrot and sweet potato and sweat for 5 minutes. Then add all the remaining ingredients apart from the crumble ingredients. Season, then cook for 10–12 minutes before removing from the heat. Transfer to an ovenproof casserole dish.

- In a bowl, add the wholemeal flour and the butter. Rub until you form a texture similar to breadcrumbs. Add the oats, breadcrumbs, seeds and Parmesan and season well. Evenly cover the vegetable mixture with the crumble mix.

- Turn the halogen oven on to 200°C and place the crumble on the high rack. Cook for 25–30 minutes until golden and bubbling.

- Serve immediately with a green salad.

- Vegetarian

Desserts

We all love desserts! Here is a selection of recipes which I hope will tempt you. Crumbles, bettys, bread and butter puddings, fruit cobblers and Eve's Pudding all work so well in the halogen. Use the recipes as a guide and change the fruit combinations to suit the seasons.

Serves 2–3

Pear, Apple and Blueberry Roast

Ingredients:
2–3 ripe pears, peeled, halved and cored
2 eating apples, peeled, cored and cut into thick wedges
2 oranges, peeled, pith removed and cut into thick wedges
4–6 tablespoons elderflower cordial
2 tablespoons dark brown sugar
50g butter
75g blueberries

This is really easy but tastes amazing. Use any leftovers to sweeten your porridge at breakfast time.

- Place the pears, apples and oranges in a roasting/baking tin, evenly distributed.

- Drizzle 4 tablespoons cordial over the fruit. Sprinkle with the brown sugar and evenly dot with the butter.

- Place in the halogen on the low rack and set the temperature to 180°C. Cook for 10 minutes. Carefully remove and drizzle the juice that has formed back over the fruit. Place back in the oven and cook for another 10 minutes.

- Remove again and drizzle with the juice, or if there's not enough, add a few more tablespoons of elderflower cordial. Sprinkle with the blueberries and place back in the oven for another 5–10 minutes.

- Serve hot or cold.

Desserts

Serves 4–6

Gooseberry Betty

Preparation time:
10 minutes
Cooking time:
30–35 minutes

I adore the taste of gooseberries and this makes a wonderfully satisfying dessert. It is a great variation on the standard fruit crumble.

- Place the gooseberries in an ovenproof dish. Sprinkle with the sugar and water. Place in the halogen on the low rack, set to 190°C and cook for 10 minutes.

- Stir and press the gooseberries slightly to help 'burst' them a little. Cook for another 5 minutes before removing from the oven.

- While the gooseberries are cooking, combine the breadcrumbs, oats and cinnamon powder. Place this mixture over the top of the fruit.

- Place the butter and syrup in an ovenproof dish and melt using the heat from the halogen oven – do not allow it to burn. Once melted, pour over the crumble mixture.

- Return the gooseberry betty to the halogen on the low rack. Cook for another 15–20 minutes until the top is golden.

- Serve with a dollop of crème fraîche or vanilla ice-cream.

Ingredients:
750g gooseberries
1–2 tablespoons sugar
1–2 tablespoons water
125g breadcrumbs
50g oats
2 teaspoons cinnamon
   powder
100g butter
3 tablespoons golden syrup

Serves 4–6

Winter Spice Crumble

Ingredients:
600g chopped fruit (I use
    rhubarb, Bramley apples
    and plums or apple mixed
    with frozen forest fruits)
50g sugar
200ml red wine
100ml orange juice
3 teaspoons cinnamon
1 teaspoon allspice
150ml plain flour
50g oats
1 teaspoon mixed spice
75g butter
50g brown sugar
40g sliced almonds

If you love the flavour of cinnamon and allspice, this is the pudding for you. Delicious served with vanilla ice-cream.

- Place the fruit in a saucepan and add the sugar, wine and orange juice. Cook gently for 5–8 minutes to start softening the fruit.

- Mix in the spices and stir well, pressing the fruit a little with your spoon to help break/soften it.

- Pour this into an ovenproof dish, making sure it fits well in your halogen oven.

- In a bowl, combine the flour, oats and mixed spice. Add the butter and rub until it forms a texture similar to breadcrumbs. Add the sugar and almonds and combine well. Pour over the fruit base, making sure it is spread evenly.

- Place the crumble in the halogen on the low rack and cook at 180°C for 20 minutes.

- Serve with a dollop of vanilla ice-cream.

- Desserts

Serves 4–6

Chocolate, Apple and Hazelnut Betty

Preparation time:
10 minutes
Cooking time:
35 minutes

This is simply yummy!

- Place the apple slices in an ovenproof dish. Sprinkle with the sugar and water. Place in the halogen on the low rack and cook at 190°C for 10 minutes.

- Stir and cook for another 5 minutes before removing from the oven.

- While the apples are cooking, combine the breadcrumbs, oats, chopped hazelnuts, chocolate chunks and cinnamon powder. Place this mixture over the top of the fruit.

- Place the butter and syrup in an ovenproof dish and melt using the heat from the halogen oven – do not allow it to burn. Once melted, pour this mixture over the crumble mixture.

- Return the fruit betty to the low rack and cook for another 15–20 minutes until the top is golden.

- Serve with a dollop of crème fraîche or vanilla ice-cream.

Ingredients:
3 Bramley cooking apples, cored, peeled and sliced
2 tablespoons sugar
1–2 tablespoons water
125g breadcrumbs
50g oats
50g hazelnuts, chopped
75g dark chocolate chunks
2 teaspoons cinnamon powder
100g butter
3 tablespoons golden syrup

Serves 4–6

Berry Ripple Mousse with Melting Biscuits

Ingredients:
225g butter
50g icing sugar
½ teaspoon vanilla essence
175g self-raising flour, sifted
50g cornflour, sifted
250g strawberries
100g raspberries
2 tablespoons caster sugar
75g cream cheese
150g double cream
100g Greek yoghurt
1 teaspoon vanilla extract

I love this pudding and I always make more biscuits as they are a real favourite in our house.

- Beat the butter and icing sugar together. Add the vanilla essence and combine.

- Combine the sifted flour and cornflour and fold in.

- Place baking parchment on a baking tray. Using a teaspoon, place dollops of the mixture evenly over the tray.

- Bake at 180°C on the low rack for 10–12 minutes until golden and just firm but not hard.

- Remove from the oven and leave on the tray for a couple of minutes before placing on a cooling rack.

- Place two-thirds of the strawberries and raspberries in an ovenproof dish. Sprinkle with the caster sugar.

- Place in the halogen on the high rack and cook at 180°C for 5 minutes. Remove and leave to one side to cool.

- Meanwhile, mix the cream cheese, double cream, yoghurt and vanilla extract together. Fold in half the cooked berries.

- Place some of the fresh fruit in the bottom of individual serving glasses. Top with a little of the yoghurt mixture, followed by the cooked berries and repeat until you almost fill each glass. Finish with the fresh berries.

- Serve with 3 or 4 cooked biscuits per serving.

- **Desserts**

Serves 2–4

Honey Grilled Figs

Preparation time:
5 minutes
Cooking time:
5 minutes

So simple, yet so delicious.

Ingredients:
2–4 figs, cut in half
Honey
Icing sugar

- Place the halved figs on a baking tray. Drizzle with honey.

- Place on the highest rack (the grill rack) and cook at 250°C for 3–5 minutes until golden and bubbling.

- Place on a serving plate, sprinkle with icing sugar and serve with ice-cream.

Serves 4–6

Chocolate Saucy Pudding

Ingredients:
115g sugar
115g butter
2 eggs, beaten
2 tablespoons milk
1 tablespoon vanilla essence
   or paste
100g self-raising flour
2 tablespoons cocoa
300ml boiling water
2 tablespoons sugar
1 tablespoon cocoa

My mum used to make this when we were children and I rediscovered the recipe when I pinched her personal cookery notebook. We used to call this a magic pudding as the sauce is poured over the top of the cake, but during cooking it miraculously goes to the bottom. I have adapted it to suit the halogen and it works really well. You could make it in small ramekin dishes, but adjust the cooking time.

- In your mixer, beat 115g sugar and the butter together until creamy and fluffy. Gradually add the beaten eggs, milk and vanilla and mix well before adding the flour and 2 tablespoons cocoa.

- Pour into a greased ovenproof dish (or ramekin dishes) and smooth over until flat.

- In a bowl or jug, mix together the boiling water, 2 tablespoons sugar and 1 tablespoon cocoa and stir thoroughly until dissolved and lump free. Pour over the sponge mixture.

- Place in the halogen on the low rack and cook at 175°C for 40–50 minutes, until the sponge is firm to touch.

- Serve with a dollop of Greek yoghurt or crème fraîche and enjoy!

● Desserts

Serves 4–6

Apple and Cinnamon Cobbler

Preparation time:
10–15 minutes
Cooking time:
18 minutes

Apple and cinnamon are a bit like strawberries and cream – they just fit together so well.

- Place the apples, sugar, cinnamon, lemon juice and raisins in a saucepan. Add 30ml water. Cook over a medium heat until the apples start to soften, but not completely – you still want them to have some firmness.

- Meanwhile, place the sifted flour and sugar in a bowl. Rub butter into the flour until it resembles breadcrumbs.

- Add the yoghurt and vanilla essence and mix.

- Place on a floured surface and roll into a thick sausage. Cut 4–5cm pieces.

- Pour the apple mixture into an ovenproof or casserole dish (make sure it fits well in your halogen oven). Place the scones around the edge and top of the apple mixture. Coat with a little milk and a sprinkle of brown sugar.

- Place in the halogen on the low rack and cook at 200°C for 15–18 minutes until the scones are golden.

Ingredients:
4–5 Bramley cooking apples, chopped
1–2 tablespoons brown sugar (depending on desired sweetness)
1–2 teaspoons ground cinnamon
Juice of ½ lemon
50g raisins
150g self-raising flour, sifted
25g sugar
50g butter
100ml natural yoghurt
1 teaspoon vanilla essence

Serves 4–6

Blueberry Crumble

Ingredients:
450g blueberries
60g sugar
75g breadcrumbs
75g ground almonds
50g oats
60g brown sugar
100g butter
25g pecan nuts

This is really tasty, especially when served with vanilla ice-cream.

- Place the blueberries in an ovenproof dish. Sprinkle with sugar and add 3 tablespoons water.

- In a bowl, mix the breadcrumbs, ground almonds, oats and brown sugar together. Rub in the butter until you form a crumbly mixture.

- Sprinkle this over the blueberries. Finish with a scattering of pecan nuts.

- Place in the halogen on the low rack and set the temperature to 180°C. Cook for 20–25 minutes until golden and bubbling.

- Serve with a dollop of vanilla ice-cream, low fat crème fraîche or natural Greek yoghurt.

Serves 4–6

Queen of Puddings

Preparation time:
10–15 minutes
Cooking time:
45 minutes

My mum used to make this for us when we were children. Comforting puddings are enjoying a well-earned revival – so much nicer than shop-bought processed puddings.

Ingredients:
90g white bread, cubed
45g sugar
420ml milk
1 teaspoon vanilla extract or paste
45g butter
2 eggs, separated
60g caster sugar
3 tablespoons jam (I use raspberry but feel free to use whatever you prefer)

- Grease an ovenproof dish, making sure it fits well in your halogen.

- Place the cubed bread in a bowl and sprinkle with the sugar.

- Heat the milk, vanilla extract and butter to almost boiling point and then pour over the bread and sugar mixture.

- When cool, add the egg yolks and whisk until smooth. Pour this into the greased dish. Place in the halogen on the low rack and cook at 180°C for 30–35 minutes until set.

- Meanwhile, beat the egg whites until they form soft peaks, gradually adding half the caster sugar.

- Melt the jam on a low heat as you don't want to burn it. Spread over the set mixture. Top with the whisked egg whites and sprinkle with the remaining caster sugar.

- Place back in the halogen and cook for another 8–10 minutes until golden.

Serves 4–6

Pineapple Upside-down Cake

Ingredients:
150g butter
150g sugar
3 eggs, beaten
150g self-raising flour, sifted
1 teaspoon vanilla essence
50g butter
50g brown sugar
2 tablespoons golden syrup
4–6 pineapple rings
3 glace cherries, halved

A traditional family favourite that can be served as a pudding or a cake.

- In your food mixer, mix 150g butter and the sugar until golden and creamy. Gradually add the eggs and combine well.

- Fold in the sifted flour and once combined thoroughly, add the vanilla essence.

- Preheat the halogen oven using the preheat setting or set the temperature to 180°C.

- Place 50g butter, the brown sugar and syrup in an ovenproof bowl and place in the halogen. While the halogen is preheating, melt the butter, but do not let it burn.

- Thoroughly grease or line an ovenproof dish or cake tin. Place a small amount of the butter/sugar mixture into the dish then place the pineapples in the bottom with the cherries in the middle of the pineapple rings. Pour on the remaining melted butter/sugar.

- Carefully spoon on the sponge mix to cover the pineapple rings. Once completely covered, carefully smooth over the surface.

- Place on the low rack and cook until the sponge is risen, golden and springs back into shape when touched – this should take between 25 and 30 minutes.

- Desserts

- Remove from the oven. Place a plate or serving dish over the top of the cake dish and flip over so the cake sits on the plate, upside down, pineapple facing upwards.

- Serve with a dollop of crème frnaîche.

Top Tip: I love pineapple upside down cake but why not experiment with other combinations or flavours. Chocolate sponge with pears is amazing – follow the recipe but swap the pineapple for pears. In the sponge add 30g of cocoa powder and 30ml of milk to the sponge mix. Vanilla sponge with rhubarb works well and for extra yumminess you could add some strawberries. Simply add a teaspoon of vanilla extract to the sponge mixture. Place the rhubarb on the base with strawberries. One of my favourites for winter is to add some sultanas and cinnamon to the sponge mixture, pouring this over thick slices of apple. Delicious when served with custard.

Serves 4–6

Rhubarb and Strawberry Biscuit Crumbly

Ingredients:

350g rhubarb, sliced

150g strawberries (can use frozen if not in season), halved

1–2 tablespoons sugar (depending on preferred sweetness)

½ packet biscuits (I use digestives or oaty biscuits)

This is a lovely pudding, with a light crumbly topping. You can use other fruit combinations to create your own version, but this is our favourite.

- Place the prepared fruit in the bottom of an ovenproof dish. Sprinkle with the sugar and 2 tablespoons water.

- Place in the halogen on the low rack and cook at 180°C for 15 minutes to help soften the fruit.

- Meanwhile, crumble the biscuits using a food processor or place the biscuits in a bag and bash gently but firmly with the end of a rolling pin to form crumbs.

- Remove the fruit from the oven. Stir well before sprinkling the biscuit crumbs over the top to form a crumble topping. Place this back in the oven and cook for another 15 minutes.

- Serve with a dollop of crème fraîche or vanilla ice-cream.

Serves 4–6

Cheat's Ginger and Apple Layer

Such a simple dish using some store-cupboard staples. It can be thrown together in minutes – perfect for a quick and easy dessert.

- Place the diced apple in a saucepan with 2 tablespoons water and 50g brown sugar. Cook over a medium heat until the apple starts to soften, but still has bite (i.e. not puréed). Add the sultanas and cinnamon and combine well.

- Grease an ovenproof dish, making sure it fits well in the halogen.

- Crumble a layer of ginger cake in the bottom of the ovenproof dish. Over this, add a layer of apple. Repeat, finishing with a ginger cake top.

- Pour over the orange juice and zest. Sprinkle with the coconut and 1 tablespoon brown sugar.

- Place in the halogen on the low rack and cook at 180°C for 15–20 minutes.

- Serve with Butterscotch Sauce or Homemade Custard (see the following recipes) . . . delicious!

Preparation time:
10 minutes
Cooking time:
20–25 minutes

Ingredients:
700g Bramley apples, cored, peeled and diced
50g brown sugar
50g sultanas
1 teaspoon cinnamon
1 small ginger cake, crumbled
Juice and zest of 1 orange
1 tablespoon desiccated coconut
1 tablespoon brown sugar

Butterscotch Sauce

Ingredients:
60g butter
120g brown sugar
6 tablespoons golden syrup
6 tablespoons double cream

- Place the butter, brown sugar and golden syrup in an ovenproof bowl and place in the halogen on the high rack at 230°C. (Use a saucepan over a medium heat if you prefer not to use the halogen oven.) Melt together gently but don't let it burn. Stir well to combine.

- Fold in the double cream (must be double as single may curdle/separate).

- Serve hot or cold.

Serves 3–4

Homemade Custard

Ingredients:
600ml full-fat milk
4 egg yolks
4 tablespoons cornflour
3 tablespoons sugar
1 teaspoon vanilla essence

- Heat the milk until just below boiling point in a saucepan on the hob over a medium heat. Meanwhile, mix the egg yolks, cornflour and sugar together. Be careful to keep an eye on the milk to avoid it spilling over.

- Remove the milk from the heat and add the egg mixture. Use a hand whisk and stir well.

- Place back on the heat and continue to stir until the custard starts to thicken – be careful not to have the heat too high or it will burn.

- Once the custard has reached your desired thickness remove from the heat. Serve immediately.

Top Tip: If you have any custard left over, you could pour it into lolly moulds and freeze – these make delicious ice-lollies!

- Desserts

Preparation time:
10 minutes
Cooking time:
25 minutes

Pear and Dark Chocolate Granola Layer

Serves 4–6

You can use granola and mix in your own dark chocolate chips, or try Dorset Cereals' amazing dark chocolate granola cereals, though I must warn you, they are seriously addictive! This pudding is lovely hot or cold.

- Place the pears in a saucepan with 2 tablespoons water and cook over a medium heat until they start to soften. Once softened, stir in the sugar.

- Mix the granola, chocolate chips and hazelnuts together.

- In an ovenproof dish, spoon in half the pears. Cover with a layer of granola mix. Add the remaining pears in another layer and cover again with the granola mixture.

- Place in the halogen oven on the low rack and cook at 180°C for 15 minutes.

- Serve hot or cold.

Ingredients:
8 ripe pears, peeled, cored and diced
1–2 tablespoons sugar
8–12 tablespoons granola
75g dark chocolate chips (if you are not using dark chocolate granola)
2 tablespoons hazelnuts, chopped

Serves 6

Rhubarb, Elderflower and Orange Upside-down Cake

Ingredients:

3–4 sticks rhubarb, cut into chunks
1–2 tablespoons sugar (or to taste)
3 tablespoons elderflower cordial
2 tablespoons water
100g sugar
100g butter
2 eggs, beaten
120g self-raising flour
1 teaspoon orange extract
Zest of 1 orange
Icing sugar to sprinkle

These flavours go so well together.

- In a saucepan on your hob, place the rhubarb, sugar and elderflower cordial. Heat very gently until the rhubarb starts to soften but still holds its shape. If you need to add more liquid, add a tablespoon of water at a time, as you do not want this too wet.

- When soft, drain the rhubarb and place in the base of a greased cake tin. (I use a sponge tin. Use a tin with a fixed bottom or you will find the juice of the rhubarb may escape when cooking.)

- While the rhubarb is cooking, use your mixer to beat the sugar and butter together until creamy. Add the beaten eggs a little at a time, continuing to mix.

- Sift the flour into the mixture and carefully fold. Once combined completely, add the orange extract and zest, retaining some zest for sprinkling over the cake later. Spoon this mixture over the rhubarb.

- Place your cake in the halogen on the low rack and cook at 180°C for 15–20 minutes. Test to see if it is cooked – it should spring back into shape when touched and if you insert a skewer into the centre of the sponge, it should come away clean. If it needs more cooking time, check every 5 minutes.

- When you are ready to serve, turn out the cake, upside down, onto a plate. Sprinkle with icing sugar and the remaining orange zest.

- Serve with cream, crème fraîche or natural yoghurt.

- **Desserts**

Serves 4

Ginger and Elderflower Roasted Rhubarb

Preparation time:
10 minutes
Cooking time:
15 minutes

A very simple pudding which tastes amazing.

- Place the rhubarb in a non-stick or greased ovenproof dish.

- Drizzle with 3 tablespoons elderflower cordial and 2 tablespoons water. Finish with a sprinkle of brown sugar.

- Place in the halogen on the low rack. Set the temperature to 200°C and cook for 10 minutes. Check to see if the rhubarb is cooked. If not, cook at 5-minute intervals. If it looks like it is browning too much, cover with a lid or tin foil.

- While that is cooking, crush the ginger biscuits either in a processor, or place in a freezer bag and very carefully bash with a rolling pin until crumbled.

- Place the yoghurt or crème fraîche in a bowl and stir in the elderflower cordial.

- Once the rhubarb is cooked, remove from the oven and place in a single serving dish, or individual serving dishes. Sprinkle with the crumbled ginger biscuits and finish with a dollop of the flavoured yoghurt/crème fraîche.

Ingredients:
3–4 sticks rhubarb, cut into
    approx. 4–5cm lengths
3 tablespoons elderflower
    cordial
2–3 tablespoons brown sugar
60g ginger biscuits
4 tablespoons natural Greek
    yoghurt or crème fraîche
1 tablespoon elderflower
    cordial

Serves 4–6

Apple and Pear Crumble

Ingredients:
2 large cooking apples, peeled, cored and cut into equally sized chunks
2 pears, peeled, cored and cut into equally sized chunks
2–3 tablespoons sugar
100g butter
150g self-raising flour
75g brown sugar
50g oats
30g mixed nuts (optional)
30g seed mix (pumpkin, sunflower, linseed, poppy) (optional)

A lovely crumble, with a nutty, seedy topping for those who like the added healthy crunch.

- Place the apple, pears and sugar in a saucepan. Add 5 tablespoons water and cook slowly on a low/medium heat until the fruit starts to soften but still holds its shape. Transfer to an ovenproof dish.

- In a bowl, rub the butter into the flour. Add the sugar, oats, nuts and seeds. Sprinkle this mixture over the fruit.

- Place in the halogen on the low rack. Set the temperature to 180°C and cook for 20–30 minutes, until the fruit is bubbling and everything is cooked.

- Serve with a dollop of cream or ice-cream. For the health conscious, try a dollop of natural Greek yoghurt.

- Desserts

Serves 4–6

Plum Tart Tartin

Preparation time:
10–15 minutes
Cooking time:
30–40 minutes

Make sure you keep the puff pastry very thin in this recipe. One of the downsides of the halogen is that it often undercooks pastry bases. So if you are making a pie, either use a pre-cooked pastry base or go without a base and just add a pastry top.

Ingredients:
60g butter
2–3 tablespoons brown sugar
4–5 ripe plums, halved and
    stoned
¼ pack puff pastry, rolled out
    to size and a thickness of
    2–3mm
Icing sugar to sprinkle

- Place the butter in an ovenproof dish – I use a 20cm round deep dish, but you can vary this.

- Place in the halogen on the high rack and set the temperature to 230°C. When the butter starts bubbling, add the sugar and stir well. Cook for another few minutes and it should start to caramelise. Don't let this burn.

- Once it looks golden, carefully add the plums, cut-side up. Fill the whole dish, making sure the plums all fit securely.

- Over the top of the plums place your rolled-out puff pastry. I don't cut off the excess pastry, I simply roll it back around the edges to form a thicker crust, but this is up to you.

- Place back on the high rack and cook at 210°C for 20–30 minutes, or until the pastry is golden and cooked.

- Leave to stand for 5 minutes before turning upside down onto a plate. The easiest way to do this is to place the serving plate upside down on top of the dish and simply flip over, holding both dishes tightly. Be careful, as the juice and sugar can burn when very hot.

- Sprinkle with icing sugar and serve with cream, crème fraîche or natural yoghurt.

Preparation time:
15 minutes

Cooking time:
30 minutes

Serves 4–6

Marmalade, Cointreau and Orange Bread and Butter Pudding

Ingredients:

8 slices white bread, ideally slightly stale

Butter for spreading on the bread

Marmalade for spreading on the bread

2–3 tablespoons brown sugar

40g sultanas

Zest of 1 orange

325ml milk

75ml double cream

2 eggs, beaten

2 tablespoons Cointreau

This is one of my favourite puddings, but as it is quite calorific it is definitely a treat rather than a daily pud!

- Spread butter on both sides of the bread, but spread the marmalade, quite thickly, only one one side. Cut the bread into triangles as this makes it more attractive and easier to place in the dish.

- Layer the bread in a greased ovenproof dish, overlapping where you can. Intersperse the layers with a sprinkle of brown sugar and some sultanas.

- In a jug, add the orange zest, milk, cream, eggs and Cointreau. Mix well.

- Pour this mixture into the ovenproof dish, pressing the bread down gently to absorb the liquid. Leave to stand for at least 20 minutes.

- When you are ready to cook, place the pudding in the halogen on the low rack. Set the temperature to 190°C and cook for 20–30 minutes, until golden.

- Serve immediately. For extra naughtiness, mix some Cointreau with double cream and serve with a generous dollop.

- Desserts

Serves 4–6

Rhubarb and Strawberry Crumble

Preparation time:
10 minutes
Cooking time:
40 minutes

I love rhubarb and strawberries. Leave the strawberries whole otherwise they will disappear into the fruit and you won't get the contrasting taste.

- Place the rhubarb in a saucepan and add the sugar and 5 tablespoons water. Cook on a low/medium heat until the rhubarb starts to soften, but still holds its shape.

- Stir in the strawberries and remove from the hob. Pour the mixture into an ovenproof dish.

- In a bowl, rub the butter into the flour. Add the oats and sugar and combine well. Sprinkle this mixture over the rhubarb and strawberries.

- Place in the halogen on the low rack and cook at 190°C for 20–30 minutes.

- Serve with cream, ice-cream, crème fraîche or, for the health conscious, natural yoghurt.

Ingredients:
3 sticks rhubarb, cut into
    2–3cm lengths
2–3 tablespoons sugar
100g strawberries, left whole
100g butter
150g self-raising flour
50g oats
75g sugar

Berry Nice Bread and Butter Pudding

Preparation time:
10–15 minutes

Cooking time:
30 minutes

Ingredients:
4–5 slices white bread, ideally
 slightly stale
Butter to spread on the bread
1 egg, beaten
150ml milk
50ml double cream
250g mixed berries
1–2 tablespoons brown sugar

There is no reason why you have to make bread and butter pudding with just sultanas and raisins – this berry combination works really well.

- Butter the bread on both sides. Choose a tray with sides that are at least 4–5cm deep and lay the bread on it.

- Mix the egg, milk and cream together. Pour this over the bread and leave for at least 20 minutes.

- Place the mixed berries in the bottom of an ovenproof dish. If you like things very sweet you could add a tablespoon of sugar, though I find I don't really need it.

- Place the soaked bread over the top of the fruit, trying to layer it if you can and sprinkling a little brown sugar between each layer.

- Place in the halogen on the low rack. Set the temperature to 180°C and cook for 20–30 minutes until golden.

- Serve warm with cream or natural yoghurt.

Desserts

Makes 6–10 depending on case size

Mini Hot Apple Muffins

Preparation time:
15 minutes

Cooking time:
20 minutes

The smell of hot apple cakes is always so tempting. These are individual little cakes which you can eat hot or cold – delicious.

Ingredients:
100g butter
100g sugar
2 eggs, beaten
120g self-raising flour, sifted
1 cooking apple, peeled, cored
    and diced
½ teaspoon ground cinnamon

- Beat the butter and sugar together until creamy.

- Add the beaten egg and continue to beat well.

- Add the sifted flour, folding in carefully. Once combined, add the apple and cinnamon and stir again.

- Place the mixture into individual muffin cases. Use silicon cases as they hold their shape – paper ones will flatten when the mixture starts to heat.

- Place the cases on a baking tray and place in the halogen on the low rack. Set the temperature to 190°C and cook for 12–18 minutes depending on the size of the cases. When the muffins are cooked they will be golden and will bounce back if gently pressed.

- Turn them out immediately onto a serving dish and serve with a dollop of cream, custard or, for the health conscious, some natural Greek yoghurt.

Serves 4–6

Eve's Pudding

Ingredients:
2–3 cooking apples, peeled,
   cored and sliced
1 tablespoon sugar
100g butter
100g sugar
2 eggs
120g self-raising flour
½ teaspoon baking powder
1 teaspoon vanilla extract

A simple, traditional pudding that kids love.

- Place the apple in a saucepan with 1 tablespoon sugar and a little water (approx. 75–100ml). Cook on a low/medium heat until the apple starts to soften.

- Then remove from the heat and place in the base of an ovenproof dish. Smooth the surface to form a flat top.

- Meanwhile, beat the butter and 100g sugar together until light and creamy. Add the eggs and continue to beat.

- Sift the flour and baking powder and add to the mixture, folding in gently. Once combined, add the vanilla extract and stir.

- Carefully dollop the cake mixture over the apple. If you can, spread gently to flatten the top.

- Place the dish in the halogen on the low rack. Set the temperature to 190°C and cook for 15–20 minutes. Check to see if the cake is done – it should spring back into shape when pressed gently. Allow extra cooking time if necessary.

- Serve warm with custard.

- Desserts

Apple, Sultana and Cinnamon Mini Cakes

Preparation time:
15 minutes
Cooking time:
20 minutes

These are a little lighter than traditional sponge puddings but so tempting. Serve them with homemade custard (see the recipe on p. 138).

Ingredients:
55g butter
55g sugar
1 egg, beaten
55g self-raising flour
1 teaspoon cinnamon
20g sultanas
50g stewed apple

- Cream the butter and sugar together until pale and fluffy. Add the egg a little at a time and continue to beat well.

- Sift the flour and cinnamon and fold into the mixture gently. Add the sultanas and combine well.

- When thoroughly mixed, half fill silicon cupcake cases with the mixture. (I have not been able to find a round muffin tray so I use silicon muffin cases and place these on the halogen baking trays that come with the accessory packs.) Press the cake mixture down to ensure the bottom of the silicon cases are covered.

- Using a teaspoon, place a spoonful of stewed apple in the centre of each case. Finish with the remaining cake mixture.

- Place in the halogen on the low rack and cook for 12–18 minutes. The cakes should be firm and spring back when touched.

- Serve warm with some custard.

Preparation time:
10 minutes

Cooking time:
25–30 minutes

Serves 4–6

Summer Fruit Cobbler

Ingredients:
400g frozen summer fruits
2 eating apples or ripe pears,
    peeled, cored and diced
2 tablespoons sugar

Scone mix
250g self-raising flour
50g butter
50g sugar
100ml buttermilk
1 egg
Beaten egg or milk for
    brushing

Feel free to use frozen fruit for this dish – a pack of summer berries mixed with a couple of eating apples or pears is perfect. The scones take minutes to make and, as the scone mix is divine, you might want to double up the recipe and also make some fresh scones. If you do make scones, add some sultanas, blueberries or cheese to the mixture – delicious!

- Place the summer fruits and apple or pear in an ovenproof dish (the same dish you will make the cobbler in) and sprinkle with 2 tablespoons sugar.

- Place in the halogen on the low rack. Set the temperature to 180°C and cook for 5 minutes. Then remove from the oven and leave to one side.

- Meanwhile, place the flour and butter in a bowl and rub together to form breadcrumbs. Add 50g sugar and combine well. (If you are making scones, add approximately 50g fruit or cheese now.)

- Mix the buttermilk and egg together and pour this mixture into the flour. Combine well to form a dough.

- Roll out on a floured surface. Cut into rounds using a pastry cutter and place on top of the summer fruits. Brush the top of the scones with a little beaten egg or milk.

- Place in the halogen on the low rack and cook at 200°C for 15–20 minutes, until the scones are golden.

- Serve immediately with custard, cream, yoghurt or ice-cream.

- Desserts

Serves 2–4

Golden Nectarines with Raspberries

This is a really simple dish that takes minutes to prepare and tastes delicious. Serve with ice-cream or vanilla yoghurt.

- Cut the nectarines in half, remove the stones and drizzle with a little honey.

- Place in the halogen on the highest rack (grill rack ideally) and set the temperature to 240°C. Grill for 3–4 minutes until the nectarines start to darken – do not walk away as they could easily burn.

- Remove from the oven and place on serving dishes with a handful of raspberries. Sprinkle some icing sugar over the nectarines.

- Drizzle some balsamic glaze over the side of the plate before serving with cream, ice-cream or vanilla yoghurt.

Preparation time:
5 minutes
Cooking time:
5 minutes

Ingredients:
2–4 nectarines
Honey
Icing sugar
Balsamic glaze
Handful of fresh raspberries

Index

THE HEALTHY LIFESTYLE DIET COOKBOOK
SARAH FLOWER

Tired of fad diets and yo-yo dieting? Do you want to lose weight and improve your health but still enjoy your food? Nutritionist Sarah Flower believes that by following the recipes in her book you can eat well, lose weight, feel better AND stay that way. Sarah's focus is on healthy eating and delicious food that all the family will enjoy. She also describes lifestyle changes that everyone can adopt to lay the foundations for healthy eating and to lose unwanted pounds if they need to. Sarah also includes superfoods, menu plans and some food swap suggestions.

ISBN 978-1-905862-74-0

EAT WELL, SPEND LESS
The complete money-saving guide to everyday cooking
SARAH FLOWER

This invaluable book contains over 200 great family recipes for busy cooks who want to save time and money, but also deliver wholesome food for their families. It's also an essential housekeeper's guide for the 21st century. Nutritionist Sarah Flower shows you how to feed yourself and your family a healthy balanced diet without spending hours in the kitchen and a fortune in the supermarket.

ISBN 978-1-905862-83-2

EVERYDAY THAI COOKING
Easy, authentic recipes from Thailand to cook at home for friends and family
SIRIPAN AKVANICH

Everyday Thai Cooking brings you the secrets of cooking delicious Thai food straight from Thailand. Author Siripan Akvanich draws on her years of experience of cooking for her restaurant customers in Thailand to enable you to create authentic Thai dishes, ranging from curries and meat and fish dishes to wonderful Thai desserts. With clear instructions and insider tips, Siripan helps you bring these dishes – many of them traditional family recipes – to life and shows you how to make them *a-roi* (delicious)!

ISBN 978-1-905862-85-6

EVERYDAY COOKING FOR ONE
Imaginative, delicious and healthy recipes that make cooking for one fun
WENDY HOBSON

Here is a collection of simple, tasty meals – specially designed for one – that can help you enjoy your everyday eating. Starting with sensible tips for shopping and for stocking your food cupboard, you'll find recipes for everything from snacks to delicious fish; and meat and vegetable main courses that keep an eye on a healthy dietary balance – and a healthy bank balance. And there's a unique feature, too. Some recipes just don't work in small quantities, and that could include some of your favourites. So we've included some of those recipes – like casseroles, roasts and cakes – and shown you how to create four different meals from one single cooking session.

ISBN 978-1-905862-94-8

How To Books are available through all good high street and on-line bookshops, or you can order direct from us through Grantham Book Services.

Tel: +44 (0)1476 541080
Fax: +44 (0)1476 541061
Email: orders@gbs.tbs-ltd.co.uk

Or via our website

www.howtobooks.co.uk

To order via any of these methods please quote the title(s) of the book(s) and your credit card number together with its expiry date.

For further information about our books and catalogue, please contact:

How To Books
Spring Hill House
Spring Hill Road
Begbroke
Oxford
OX5 1RX

Visit our web site at

www.howtobooks.co.uk

Or you can contact us by email at info@howtobooks.co.uk

Like our Facebook page How To Books & Spring Hill

Follow us on Twitter @Howtobooksltd

Read our books online www.howto.co.uk